CEO Of My SOUL

CEO Of My SOUL

The Self-Love Journey Of A
Small Business Owner

Nic Cober, Esquire
CJ Publishing

For information contact: CJ Publishing, a division of Cober Johnson, LLC, 2200 Pennsylvania Avenue, NW, 4th Floor East, Washington, DC 20037, info@cjrlegal.com, or www.niccober.com

Book and Cover design by CJ Publishing. Cover photo by Cedric Terrell; Song lyrics reprinted: 1983: "We're Going All The Way", Jeffery Osborne (A&M); 1976 "Mr. Melody", Natalie Cole (Capitol); 1981 "Under Pressure" Queen and David Bowie (EMI). ISBN: 123456789 First Edition: March 2016 10 9 8 7 6 5 4 3 2 1

To God: Thank You for being THE inspired co-author in my life and this book. I am so grateful for this amazing journey we are on!

To My Parents: Barbara and Andre. Thank you for providing me with a beautiful childhood and past.

To My Children: Jordan and Logan. Thank you for being my inspired present.

To Harold: Thank you for being my beloved partner as we take this journey into our amazing future.

CONTENTS

PART FOUR-EXPAND.

PROLOGUE

"Welcome to the Jungle!"
-Guns N' Roses

The media often poses the question, particularly to women: *"Can you have it ALL?"* Or even better: *"How do you maintain work/life balance?"* As a young entrepreneur, mother and (on-again, off-again) wife, I struggled daily (and most times, hourly) with how to prioritize the responsibilities in my life. That is why I was compelled to tell my story. You see, I began writing this book about my life as an entrepreneur in 2010, soon after I unceremoniously closed the doors of my eight-year-old business for the final time.

When I read books, watched interviews or skimmed articles about business owners, I noticed that rare is the person who takes you behind the scenes. Most people gloss over the failures (bankruptcies, divorces, etc.) and highlight their tremendous successes. However, I believe that there are important lessons in the valleys of life, and that was the intention behind the creation of this book.

I owned and operated a small business in the Washington, DC area called *Soul Day Spa and Salon*. At the peak of my success, I had two locations, thirty team members, and a nationally recognized and acclaimed brand. Personally, I had two amazing sons, was married, and had my dream home in Falls Church, Virginia, a suburb of Washington, DC with outstanding schools -- something I valued immensely. If you were to take a snapshot of my life at that time, it was objectively enviable. However, within two years, my *"Fantasy Island"* of a life collapsed leaving me bankrupt after closing both locations, divorced (again) and questioning my own soul (the pun is very much intended).

Work. Life. Balance. Small Business. Relationships. Self-Love. My story uses the backdrop of the small business world to discuss these important life lessons. This is not just a book about how to open and operate a business, although you will learn how I did it. Similarly, this is not just a book about relationships, although there are lessons to be learned there as well. *CEO of My Soul* is a journey, which is ultimately a spiritual one, on how to learn your life's purpose and how to find the strength to love yourself even at the most painful and inconvenient times.

I consider you a friend. You've picked up my book, and I am grateful to you in advance for that. I will share both personal and business stories that will provide context for who I am and the decisions that led me to open, operate and finally close my businesses. I will also share personal stories about my childhood, my family and my relationships, because ultimately, they were catalysts for my business decisions—for better and for worse. This is not a *"Real Housewives"* episode though, boo. First of all, I'm an attorney and with all candor, my memory and my exes' memories may be different, especially on "bad" facts, and your girl is not trying to get sued! In all seriousness though, there is no healing when you are exclusively blaming others. The most valuable lesson that came out of writing this book was self-acceptance. I have the courage to acknowledge my own decisions and mistakes, not run away from them. That's where the magic happens.

On each page of this book, I promise to tell the truth and take responsibility for all my decisions, and I will even step out of the narrative to say—hey girl! I really screwed up here—don't do it! Think of it as a cross between a *"For Dummies"* and a *"Girlfriend's Guide"* to business and life—all rolled into one. I will give you "green flags," "yellow flags" and "red flags" that you should take as "do this right here!" "slow your roll—get a second opinion" and "damn. Damn. DAMN!" (That's my Florida Evans voice from the historic Black sitcom *"Good Times."* Look it up if you haven't seen it. I make a bunch of random Black pop culture comments—the book will be immensely funnier when you can flow!)

Every experience is different, but there are some universal truths that lil' mom and pop business people either don't know or don't have the resources to follow. I'll share what I learned. It's fine to tell you don't do this or that, but here, I will have you walk down that road with me. You'll see the choices I had before me. You'll see the reasons why I made the good, the bad, and the downright wretched decisions when I did. It is really a story about growing up and learning powerful lessons—about business, life and our deeply rooted power within. Through it all, I faced divorces, business closings AND the IRS, and not only survived, but thrived. I've said it before; I had to lose my Soul (the business) to find my own. So, let's begin.

PART One
ENVISION.

CHAPTER One

The Conception of Soul
My Work-Life Imbalance

2001 was an important year for me and an appropriate place to start the story of Soul and how I became an entrepreneur. It was the year I turned 30, and it was my fourth year practicing law at one of the largest and most prestigious firms in Washington, DC. I had a gorgeous four-year-old son, Jason. After a recent divorce, I had purchased my first townhouse a couple of years earlier, and to reward myself for all of my hard work, I treated myself to a midnight blue Mercedes Benz CLK-320 for my birthday. Objectively, these were all noteworthy accomplishments, and given the fact that I was also a young Black girl from Oakland, California and the first lawyer in my family, my accomplishments seemed to take on a slightly larger importance for someone with my humble background.

However, because my name was Nicole from The Town, and not "Cinderella," "Belle," "Princess Tiana" or any happily ever after character from Disneyland, it was only half the story. In reality, each day of that year, I was faced with two foreboding fears: 1.Would I be fired for incompetence at the law firm and therefore be unable to financially provide for my son; and 2. Would I lose custody of my son because of the demands my career placed on me.

That was the predicament I found myself in. Paradox? Irony? Tragic comedy? I don't know which words most accurately describe how I was living that year, but "petrified" was the second-to-second emotion I was feeling. Clarence (ex #1, i.e. foreshadowing) and I had been in a brutal custody battle over Jason since our divorce a couple of years earlier. He lived in Maryland and had opened a day care center after years of running his grandmother's childcare business. We started off with joint custody of Jason, but when I moved to Alexandria, Virginia to receive the advantages of an award-winning public school system, he challenged me for full custody. He argued that he was a better parent than I was because my schedule as a "high-powered attorney" prevented me from properly caring for my son. I know we are now in the "*Lean In*" era where women are doing superhuman things like climbing Mount Everest during childbirth, but things were a bit tough on me. Divorced. Attorney. Mom. I just didn't fit anywhere very well.

. . .

Let me step back a bit, and tell you how I got to DC (and divorced) in the first daggone place. In May of

1993, I was about to graduate from UC Berkeley (yay!) but with no job or post graduate prospects (boo!). My heart's desire was to be a journalist, but my head's desire was to make some money. I hedged my bets and took the LSAT, the test to get into law school. In short, my test scores sucked, so while everyone around me was being admitted into prestigious grad school programs, I was sitting in my canary yellow colored childhood bedroom at my folk's crib in a constant state of panic because I still hadn't been accepted anywhere. All that changed overnight in the latter part of the summer. I found out that Howard University School of Law had moved me off their waitlist to their "get-your-behind-from-California-to-Washington-DC-in-48-hours-and-start-school" list. I didn't think twice about it. I packed up my jeans, sneakers and a few pictures and my parents took me to Oakland airport on a Saturday afternoon. I started school the next week.

When I got to DC, it was a tremendous culture shock. Think *"Livin' For the City"* by Stevie Wonder, shock. You know at the end of the song, when they do a sad little skit about a fella stepping off the bus in "New York" looking around at the "skyscrapers and every thang?" Yep, that was kind of me (except without getting wrongfully convicted for a drug bust! Dang, Stevie!) I went from the womb of security that was my home, family and friends to total and complete fear, instability and strangers in Chocolate City. I started with nothing: no money, no family, no food, and no knowledge about the area. For example, I was completely unprepared for the weather—I had like one little windbreaker and no socks when winter showed up. And while DC in 1993 was not quite the "Murder Capital," it was still rough. Remember now, your girl had lived at home with her parents in the affluent suburban hills of Oakland up until last Friday, so it was a dramatic change to hear all the sirens whizzing around me when I made it to the Nation's capital.

But I was thrown a life line, of sorts. The new dean of the law school was Judge Arnold Jackson, my father's former boss in Alameda County Superior Court. He was a tall, stoic, regal Black man with a personality that matched all his credentials...formal. Not really one for jokes and small talk. He was charged with rebuilding the law school's reputation and infrastructure, both of which had taken a bit of a beating for a few years. He had great respect for my dad, and while I could never prove that he stood up for me with his admissions office, it was always a thought in the back of my mind.

Until my tuition checks came in to give me some other living options, I stayed with...the Dean and his daughter, who was in college at the time. Can you imagine the shear intimidation and stress that was on me at the time? Dear Lord, I was freaked out. I mostly stayed in my room, studied and ate boxes of Wheat Thins because I was too nervous to talk to either of them. (I nearly lost 10 pounds by winter's break.) Plus, I desperately needed to prove that I deserved to be at the school, after all the Dean had (maybe? possibly?) done for me.

Further, I was insanely homesick. No. There needs to be another word. How about home-ICU or home-hospice? Yep, those are closer fits. Those first months were terrible. Just terrible. Lonely. And to top it all off, I was stressed out about what the hell a "contract" or a "tort" even was. Pitiful. I didn't realize how traumatic leaving home for the first time would be. I'll tell you about my parents in a little while, but, they were my peeps! I missed them so much. I tried not to cry when I was on the phone with them so they wouldn't worry. And I was never Ms. Social Butterfly, even at home, so I didn't know how to make friends easily. So now my girlfriends (all 5 of them) were away and my little boyfriend at the time had chosen another law school to attend. That meant for a while the only people I came into contact with was the Dean....and the daughter. I felt like a baby being born via C-section — just yanked out into a cold ass world. So, like that baby, I cried...a lot.

Which leads me to my first marriage, indirectly. DC and I were not a love connection. At all. While my tuition money eventually came in and I got out of my much appreciated yet highly uncomfortable living quarters, I just never felt like I fit in. I found the law school to be kind of cliquish. And while I made some nice friends, I pretty much kept to myself. But I did find a best friend in my new boyfriend, Marcus, from Rocky Mount, North Carolina. (He was so proud of his little town!) We met in class during our first year at Howard. He was such a genuine and kindhearted guy. While most people I met were "cool," professional and ambitious, he was jolly and loving. He was a bit of a fish out of water too, so we were two peas in a pod.

By way of background, I was always that "relationship girl." From waaay back. I'll tell you more soon, but for instance, I had one boyfriend in high school, one for most of college, one the last year of college and one in law school. And they were all very stable, positive, and loving relationships. In fact, at that time, I couldn't remember when I was *not* in a relationship. Studying and being a girlfriend were pretty much my full time gigs. When Marcus and I broke up our last year in law school, it wasn't for any nefarious reason. I think it had just run its course. He and I were more like buddies by then. He was definitely my security blanket a wonderful friend. Soon after, however, I met Clarence.

To this day, I still have very little to say about him. We did not mix at all! How did we get together? Well, when I did go out, I liked to dance, so we actually met at a club. We started dating, and I found him to be very paternalistic, and in the beginning, I was very nice and naïve—almost childlike. He seemed to like taking care of me, in a fatherly way and his family was (and still is) very kind to me. I still missed my family, and I guess maybe Clarence's family (and he) filled a void that started to develop when I got to DC. Yeah, but that dynamic wore off fast. Once I graduated from law school, we argued more and more. But strangely enough, he asked me to marry him. I think he really just wanted a family because he was always telling me what a great mother I would be, which was odd, I thought. Not *"I love you"* or *"I want to spend the rest of my life with you,"* but, *"you will be a great mom,"* like I was a breeding maternal mammal or something. Maybe it was the daycare thing, I thought.

I think he also suspected that as soon as I passed the California Bar, I might leave. And he would have been right. When he proposed, I kept saying: *"Really? Are you sure?" "Are you serious?"* I did not want to marry him. I knew that. But, I just couldn't see, at the time, saying "no" because I didn't want to hurt his feelings. [I know! I know! Stop yelling at your electronic device or the book, ok?]. Well, I thought, we would have a looong engagement, and I can see if we can work on some of our personality conflicts. But, as fate would have it, I found out I was preggers the day before I was sworn in for the Bar, in November 1996. And I never considered having a child and not being married or any other option. We were married in January 1997, and Jason was born in July. Clarence and I had a disastrous year, and as I found my voice and my courage, I moved out in July 1998.

. . .

Over the next few years, we would be in court for dozens of issues surrounding Jason. Then in 2001, we had one of our many hearings — this one was to establish where Jason would attend preschool and where he would live. While I could think of 1,000 reasons why living with me in Alexandria would be best for Jason, the senior gentleman judge who heard our case had a sympathetic ear for the ex's argument.

The words he uttered that day would literally change the trajectory of my life forever: *"If I had to make a final decision today on the issue of custody, I would give the child to the father and the mother would have visitation on the weekends because of the demands of her work schedule..."* I went numb. *"Give." "The Child." "To the Father!?"* The court really made remarkable assumptions that I could not walk and chew gum at the same time. Or work and be an able parent. I was young. I was scared. I was devastated.

Let's pause here for the classic literary lesson of the day. For all you high school English Lit connoisseurs: Remember the short story, *"The Gift of the Magi,"* by O. Henry? I'm a romantic at heart, so I loved it. It was the story of a new couple. Essentially, they are very much in love and very...broke. Christmas was coming up, and they each wanted to get the other a wonderful gift. The wife, unbeknownst to her hubby, knows he loves his pocket watch. She cuts off her long flowing hair to buy him an accessory for his treasured heirloom. Meanwhile, the husband pawns his pocket watch for some loot to purchase a beautiful hair comb for his sweetie. Educators across the land have used this love story as an example of how to explain the literary device of "irony." Well, thanks to me, you have a more modern and depressing example of it.

It appeared that I was at risk of losing my son because I was a "high-powered" attorney. But in reality, I was not high, and I had no power. Since the day I stepped my stilettos into that office, I was battling my ex. We would disagree about everything: school selection, healthcare, childcare, sleeping habits, clothes—everything divorced people with children could possibly argue about. The enormity of the situation impacted my work productivity and focus. Law firms deal in billable hours like the blackjack dealers deal hearts and diamonds. And the more I was out of the office for court battles and commutes, the less time I could devote to my work assignments. For example, I commuted about 30 miles from Alexandria, Virginia to Jason's daycare center—which happened to be his father's in-home daycare in Laurel, MD. I would then drive from Laurel to the law firm in Washington, DC and back again in the evening. Too bad you cannot collect frequent flyer miles on Interstate 495 because your girl was On. The. Go.

My colleagues and bosses were understanding and compassionate, to a point. And that point came in November of 2001. That was when they called me in for my performance evaluation. *"Nicole, we think it's time you consider other employment options. We will give you six months and keep you on here at a reduced salary in order to give you time to find another job."*

You see the "irony"? *Oh, the "The Gift of the Magi"* of it all! In my story, however, there were no gifts or love—just loss and suffering. On the one hand, I was portrayed as this ambitious woman who put her career before her child, and on the other hand, I was an underperforming entry-level attorney who didn't devote enough energy to her professional advancement. Really?

Dude, seriously? And all at the ripe old age of 30. What's more was that I had no support system or shoulder to cry on at that time. My parents were still in California. My friends either were single and successful or married and seemingly stable. I didn't think anyone would truly understand what I was going through. I was scared, ashamed and felt like the loneliest little girl in the world.

. . .

Thus, on this day in November of 2001, I was "let go"...albeit slowly. Before I could face my demise or redemption (I wasn't sure which yet) I had to answer one question: How the hell was I going to remove myself from this dimly lit conference room of career assassination? The mission was very short and succinct: Get to the nearest bathroom stall. That, if accomplished successfully, would be a noteworthy task, indeed. How can I describe how I left the office that day? I wish "surreal" wasn't so overused.

But, I was trapped with limited options available. Should I: A) Fake it and pull out my inner Naomi Campbell diva, and then strut the runway where my audience consisted of secretaries, paralegals and messengers who would all be reading my eyes and body language for any indication of termination. Or should I: B) Be an example of defeat and imitate the homies on death row in any Hollywood production, a la Sean Penn's *"Dead Man Walking"* style? At that point, I was so numb that I could not physically feel my legs. I had no time for any emotional drama or defeat—I just concentrated very carefully on getting to the damn bathroom without collapsing—like a happy hour bar patron at 9:01pm on a Thursday night. Sometimes "barely making it" is enough.

When I reached my destination, I got to the stall, quietly closed the door and gently sat down on the toilet, with my skirt still neatly intact. I just sat there pondering the complete and utter failure which had become my life. For the record, I apparently sucked at both being a mother and an attorney. Oh, and a wife. Even though I left a marriage that I should have never been in to begin with, on the record, I failed at that too. I mean, really? Who is divorced before she is 30 years old? Strike one. And labeled an "ambitious, never around" mom. Strike two. And to round out the self-loathing party game, I'll throw in a "Dead Wo-Man Walking Attorney," for a perfectly pitiful score! Strike three. God. I needed help. So that's what I did. I called God.

CHAPTER Two

"Dear God, It's Me, Nic."
The Mother Of Soul

Who am I? How did I get to this toilet tête-à-tête with the Almighty? At that point in my life, I was a good, Catholic girl from Oakland, California, and me and the Lord were on pleasant, yet formal terms. Religion and God were a bit different in our house than in most traditional Black households. For example, growing up, I knew my mom was...something religious. I could cheat and ask her the answer now, but I strive to be "AAAT" (i.e. Authentic At ALL Times) with you and the truth is, I still have no idea what my mom's religious affiliation is or was—and for an African-American female Baby Boomer, that is like Halley's Comet rare. My mom's religious philosophy was short and succinct: "Holy Rollers" got on her "damn nerves," because they were "damn hypocrites," but she believes in God and prays and is a good person. And that was that.

In contrast, my dad was neutral on religion growing up, but I knew he was Catholic. In fact, the Cobers were a very Black Catholic Southern family... i.e. rituals were observed and they attended mass faithfully. I got all the sacraments. I was baptized. I got my First Communion. And as an aside, I also got to go to the hairdresser for the first time to get my hair "pressed with a hot comb"...got the ears burnt up and every thang. There is no need to call Child Protective Services on Mama Barb now though. Every little coil-y-haired girl like me went through this hair hazing process. But it seems this completely barbaric ritual is almost dead--we allow our lil' puddin' cups to wear their hair natural now! But I digress.

I was also confirmed, but that was it. Oh yeah-- me and my brother attended Catholic schools for thirteen years. Though mom didn't care for religion, my dad cared deeply about Catholic education. And my mom cared about what dad cared about in that area, so...there you have it.

Growing up, I got the clear impression that being Catholic was more of a non-Black thing. I really felt left out in school when my girls were singing all the cool gospel songs they learned at their Baptist church, and I couldn't hold a note! Still bitter... But, I'll move on. Basically my dad was laid back about everything except education. He was adamant that we went to the best schools in Oakland. And he believed that those schools were Catholic schools, so my younger brother and I attended St. Elizabeth's and Bishop O'Dowd (me) and St.

Paschal's and St. Mary's (him) for years. Which ties me back to my relationship with Baby Jesus, my Lord, God.

Like I said, our relationship was a very formal, respectful, yet impersonal thing. Well, at least on my part. For example, my prayers tended to start like, "Dear God, thank you so much for all of my blessings! You are The Best. And please let me get that A in English." The older I got, I could definitely sense a theme of prayer: "Please and Thank You's" around my career. *"Please let me get into Cal!"* and *"Thank you for getting me into Howard University School of Law"* and *"Thank you for helping me pass the California bar –You ROCK, Jesus!"* While I'm sure that the big H E was prepared in advance for our toilet stool, fire-side chat, I was not.

Well, in all humility, honesty and self-reflection, I had never really failed at anything this huge. I didn't know what this actually felt like. I mean, I was the "good girl." Everyone was always proud of me. Everyone rewarded and affirmed my accomplishments. I was the B, B+ student, class VP, cheerleader, happy, sweet chick. I never smoked, did any drugs or drank. (Well, I drank wine coolers in high school during our national basketball championships, but that was pretty much it in terms of infractions. And oh yeah, I came home with a "hickey" on my neck at 16. Dad was so disappointed!)

College...it was the same boring thing. I went to the University of California at Berkeley, where I graduated in four years (which is apparently an accomplishment these days!) with dual majors in Mass Communications and Sociology because I liked the media, and I liked knowing how people interacted. I was also a member of Delta Sigma Theta, Sorority, Inc., the preeminent African American public service sorority in the United States. Most sororities are known for the social aspect of college life, but traditionally, Deltas have the (well earned) reputation for handling business on campus and in the community. Again, this was a tremendous honor...and accomplishment.

Next, on my "High-Ambition Express" was law school and, of course, I had to go and knock it out of the park there, too! Top of the class, Howard *Law Journal*, Moot Court, with a sprinkle of class Vice President on the side. Good grief. Did I mention that I passed the California Bar on the first try? This is cringe worthy... The only reason I'm even giving you this background is to let you know how utterly ill-prepared I was for this moment. (I forgot: when I finished law school, I clerked for two years with the Chief Judge of the DC Court of Appeals. Okay. I'm done!)

I'm saying that the infamous bathroom break that I was taking with Jesus was a doozy. My thoughts and mind were filled with fear, with anger, and with uncertainty. But, something in me, deep within me, spoke of hope and this was my new prayer: "*Lord, I don't know what to do. I don't know what I want. I don't know what I'm even capable of, really. But I trust You. I need You. Please help me with all this. I promise that whatever You give me, I will work hard day and night and do my best.*" Too numb to cry, I just sealed it with a Catholic "Amen," Sign of The Cross, and took a deep breath. I flushed the toilet, washed my hands, and took the rest of the day off and headed to the hair salon to drown my sorrows in the shampoo bowl.

CHAPTER Three

What's The Big Idea?

Three life lessons were drilled home for me that day. One, at some point in your life, whether it is in the beginning, middle or end, you will face failure and inequity, no matter how "good" or perfect you try to be. Two, those moments have the potential to be transformative if you allow the process to work that way. Three, maybe it's based on my family or my past performance, but even in my darkest moments, I had hope. I believed in God and my abilities. Well, I always was a bit uncertain about how strong my innate acumen was, but I worked hella hard. And I knew if God gave me a vision, a goal and/or an idea, I'd work my butt off to make it happen. There are probably a lot of other lessons, but in that moment, those were the essential tools I was equipped with.

While I knew I needed a fabulous idea, there was another ingredient in place—a sense of urgency to make a dream/idea/vision materialize. In my case, I had six months to make something happen before my firm would terminate me. 9/11 had only taken place a couple of months prior to my termination. The world was in complete chaos, it seemed. Everything that was stable and certain seemed volatile and unnerving now. A slow fire within me was smoldering and finally cracked me wide open. I think I was very receptive to change, and I definitely had the belief that it was coming very soon. Now, all I needed was the big idea.

Okay. The idea that I prayed for, from the Lord my Savior, actually came very quickly, which coincided quite nicely with my employment expiration date. Outside of working and being with my son, the place that I devoted a disproportionate amount of time in was, as fate would have it, the hair salon. The hair salon experience is a uniquely communal one, particularly for Black women. I believe God gifted us with a hair texture that ensured we would visit this collective watering hole at least once in our lives. And I can (un)safely generalize that, historically, the salon has not been a pleasant experience. [Insert your own imaginary political incorrectness brackets on these next few paragraphs, please and thank you.]

The Black hair salon. My thoughts. First, one typically can finish an amicus brief in less time (a little legal humor there!) than it takes for you to get out of a hair salon. Another generalization (okay, true stereotype) is that stylists are artists and artists are...*temperamental*. Now, I don't know if I have the license as a Black female former salon owner to say this, but, Black women do have a reputation of being...Occasionally Unpleasant. And then, with that generalization, the subcategory of stylists, is surprisingly...Accurate.

The final negative (i.e. true) stereotype about some Black hair salons is that they lacked professionalism. Exhibit A. The appearance of said stylist in rollers during work hours... Not attractive. An additional note on professionalism: Ladies: I should not be able to purchase my cell phone carrier service, a "Louie" Vuitton bag, and *the Fast and the Furious Part IX CD* all in the SAME establishment. No. Bueno. Further, it's frustrating as hell to listen to a stylist's conversation with her daycare provider on the phone. While I normally view multitasking as a valuable skill set, I am a bit unnerved when a stylist has the cell phone in one hand and is sealing my curl pattern with a heated metal object in the other!

In short, these experiences have been imprinted in my brain since I was a fetus, I'm sure. My beautifully fly mother, "Momma Barb," in my humble opinion, has always hailed as one of the most attractive women in all of Oakland, if not the World! To me, she was always my role model: Brilliance, beauty and grace personified. And her crown of glory was her Clairol colored, light ash blonde highlighted hair, which she invested a lot of time, money, and many of my formative childhood years on maintaining.

Mama Barb was born and raised in Oakland, California. She was the oldest of seven children and her earliest memories are of two things: taking care of children and cleaning the house. She went to Castlemont High School, where she was crowned the first Black homecoming queen and head cheerleader. She went into the workforce as a legal secretary where she refined my affection for perfect diction and law offices. And our home life benefited greatly from all her good grammar and cheerfulness!

Growing up, my mom was neither particularly religious nor militant. While I was from Oakland, it was always a little disappointing that the mythology of all things Black and Oakland didn't really apply to my childhood. I mean, it would be fabulous to claim that my father was one of the original Black Panthers and my mother courageously stood up to the "pigs," i.e. the police. In my mind, she carried baby Nic on one hip and her rifle on the other while she paraded through downtown Oakland and reached her final destination of feeding children at the free breakfast program center — all with her black beret strategically tilted on her foot tall Afro!

Um, no.

Instead, my father, Andre, was actually a "pig" (albeit a handsome one), otherwise known as a sheriff for Alameda County. When I went to Cal, I started exploring my scholarly – engineered, political "roots" by doing a research paper on the Black Panthers. I asked my parents if they had any ties or interests in the movement (I think I had on a dashiki that I picked up from *Urban Outfitters* or something.) I can still hear the piercing, high pitched laughter that rang in my ears and through the house. My father was sitting down reading *The Oakland Tribune* with the news on the television in the background.

"*Aw Hell naw,*" he muttered without lifting his eyes. "*I remember somebody handing out flyers for a meeting at Laney College one day,*" Andre began. "*I went and saw what them fools were talking about. The next day, and I mean the VERY next day, I went downtown and signed up for the Sheriff's department.*" I was horrified. Dreams crushed. In fact, he said the only contribution he made to the Panthers was when Huey Newton was "in the hole" (i.e. solitary confinement) and he watched out for him, "rapped with him" and gave him extra food. Good Grief! This was pathetic.

Was that it? Was that where my Panthers faux legacy would end? Hopefully not. I turned to Mama Barb. Anything? Anything? Mom give me something! "*Girl, they wanted me to stop straightening my hair and grow an Afro! Really? Not. Interested.*" And she continued stirring the spaghetti sauce or whatever. The hair. See? The story comes full circle. Hair. In my beautiful, lovingly supportive family, Barbara and Andre's focus was on me (and my little brother Brian who you will hear about later), not politics. Not religion. Just loving and educating their kids. How can I be mad at that? Right? Oh, and hair...

. . .

So, was my mother...obsessed with her hair? Yes. Yes, she was, is and will be for her entire life. Listen, if a woman says with a straight face: "*My hair color formula is Light Ash Blond. I want it to be used on my hair when I die. At my funeral. In my coffin. If it's not, I will ask permission of Jesus, who is seated at the right hand of the Father, to come back to Earth and haunt you until the end of your days. And when you get to heaven, if you are so lucky after that grave sin you committed, I will continue to kick your tail all up and through that place, capeesh?"* The statement and the facts behind it tend to leave an impression of great import on a person. Anyways, how was it that I was to open a hair salon after being canned? Maybe now you have a bit of context....

But I can't take credit for the initial idea of owning a salon. I can only take credit for being a passionate observer of the industry for thirty years. In those years, I have seen the good, bad and ratchet that existed in the industry. For example, I waited nearly eight hours one time to get my hair done for my high school prom in 1989 by one of the most popular stylists in Oakland—the late Ron Newton. (He was, ironically, the son of the late Huey P. Newton. Seriously.)

I had had some really awful experiences since, but they all ended when I met Jana, and that is where I sat on that day I was canned, in her styling chair. Jana was the dream to all my hair nightmares: She was punctual, beautiful, gracious, professional, and my hair always looked amazing—every time. We could talk about life, yet still she could get me out of the chair before nightfall, so that's where I went to drown my employment sorrows. While I sat in Jana's chair telling her about my meeting, she listened, comforted me and curled...my hair. Maybe it was that pleasant experience that I took to bed with me one night because I had a vivid dream soon after that I owned a Black Supercuts... And I had cloned Jana!

CHAPTER Four

"It Was All A Dream..."
—Biggie Smalls

Now my perfect entrepreneurial stew was simmering: I was a "workaholic" mama who needed more flexibility in my schedule so my ex couldn't swipe my kid away; I had a short-term termination plan that my kind-hearted, passive aggressive firm gave me; I had an acute acumen for the personified insanity that is otherwise known as the hair salon industry, and I had God's grace that planted a beautiful idea in my head. I was ret ta go!

Let me back up a bit because it's important — the dream. Okay, a few things. First, as I mentioned before I'm not religious. I don't get visions. I was not aware of any moments of my childhood where God really, like spoke to me. That just wasn't my experience. And I was the unusual Catholic. I mean a Christmas-and-cute-Easter-outfit, Catholic. My faith, up to that point, was a very respectful, yet formal "thank you Jesus" interaction.

I kind of felt what I imagined the "tragic mulatto" feels like: too White to be accepted by Blacks and too Black to be loved by Whites. For me, I really didn't relate to the Black religious thing or the Roman Catholic experience. I just knew I loved God, even though I was a tiny bit afraid, the way a child should be of a parent. I didn't want to do anything to really piss Him off so, can you understand how a nonreligious person like myself would feel to receive such a specific, direct, and clear answer to my bathroom prayer? I mean I can't remember the specific timing, but it was not longer than a week.

And while the dream did not include Charlton Heston and a burning bush or anything, it was pretty damn close in my world. Well, it left that kind of impression on me. It felt like an answer to me. And that's all that matters, right? What is in your mind and heart? I kind of felt that I was on a mission, okay... From God...and that I needed to make this happen. I mean, I promised Him, and I wasn't one to go back on a promise, especially to My Lord and Savior.

. . .

When I say that I am an enthusiastic person, I'm an enthusiastic person! I mean, I come from enthusiastic genes. I was a second generation cheerleader, for Jonah's sake. Also, I have entrepreneurial DNA in me. After spending several years as a sheriff and working part-time at a liquor store, my dad got enough money to purchase the business. Woo Hoo! We moved on up — like

George and Weezie—to a new house in the Oakland Hills. I guess at a very young age, I knew what it meant to "own your own business."

My dad has always been my hero. A lot of people "talk loud, and do nothing," but my father has always been a man of quiet action. Mom said one day he just said, "*I bought the liquor store.*" With regard to the house, he said, "*Let's take a ride,*" and that's when we knew we were getting a new house. Man, I love that! Further, my dad was really ahead of his time on stepping out as a business owner in Oakland. There were no small business loans being handed out. And even though some pooh-poohed owning liquor store, I thought it was awesome. And, it was a little grocery store... But also sold liquor. Or the other way around. I don't know. But all I do know is that I was proud to be an entrepreneur's child growing up.

Again, when the idea was given to me, it just seemed so natural, so perfect to me. Of course, I should own my own business. I did have initial thoughts that maybe I would be letting my parents down if I didn't go to another law firm. I mean, I didn't want their "proud parent" frequent flyer miles to expire. But, in true Cober parent fashion, they were so excited and encouraging, especially surprise! Barbara. "*Girl! You have done everything I have ever asked. Whatever you want to do is amazing. If you wanted to weave baskets, make mine the first one! You got an education to have options, not to be limited. And personally, I think a nice, upscale hair salon sounds fabulous!"* And, in true Andre Cober fashion, he said, *"Go for it. Sounds good."* Thus, the deal was set!

CHAPTER Five

The Creation of My SOUL Cookbooks, Hide and Seek & Business Plans

Once again, I had a project! And one thing you should know about your girl, she loves a damn project! I went into work the next day on a mission! I had energy! I had focus! I didn't have the nervous breakdown that could have easily been expected. No, I channeled that energy — pause. That is probably a phrase that I live by. Everyone has fear and nerves or whatever, but those who successfully defeat them know how to channel that energy into something positive. Like learning how to put together a business...

I started with the Small Business Administration's website. I remember getting a big, 3-inch binder and printing off about 200 pages... Every single section of the website. It was a hell of a book to put together. But I read and absorbed everything about the small business world from cover to cover. And the more I read and highlighted, the more gleeful I became.

I would shut my office door for eight hours a day and for days straight—time just flew by. My poor assistant Libby would occasionally poke her head in to see if I needed anything. Food? Water? Depends undies (No bathroom breaks)? It was a bit much, but I didn't care. I was obsessed, and I had little time. After reading the website information from beginning to end, I knew that I needed to start with a business plan. But at that time, there were no industry-specific templates online. I decided I had to... Gasp! Go to the library. It was 2001; the daggone Internet was only five years old.

You're probably not surprised to hear that many ideas—brilliant ideas—are taken to the grave because of two simple words: business and plan. Creative and otherwise hard-working folks hate writing. If you ask someone to *talk* about their genius idea, nine times out of ten he is on point. However, memorializing these words on paper? Crickets. Deer in headlights.

Well, I really enjoy writing, especially on topics I know about. The problem here was obvious, right? I had no clue about opening a salon or any business for that matter. Luckily for me that the other of my wonder twin powers that activate is researching. While I was admittedly mediocre with skills of a law firm, (I mean can one really be hyped up about insurance coverage litigation?) my talents seemed to work quite nicely in the business development arena. That is the zone I was in. It was what you needed to get it done. And you need to be all in. And I was.

That weekend, Jason and I spent the day at the Clara Barton library, in Alexandria, Virginia. We started, of course, in the children's section. Thomas the Train, the Bernstein Bears, you name it—our whole crew was represented. Then, as is the case when a four-year-old is your companion, it was time for a potty break. *"You did not acquire mommy's bladder of steel, my friend,"* I mused. I took his hand, and we proceeded to the back of the library for temporary bowel relief. On the way back, however, we played a little game of "hide-from-yo-mama in the cookbook section." As I followed this happy child on what started off as a wildly random act of innocent child's play, my eyes glazed across the bookshelves of cookbooks. And, in this seemingly random moment, my eyes zeroed in on a white glossy, rather elementary looking book. The writing was black, but there were pink decorations on it. A little pink blow dryer. And a little pink shampoo bowl. The book was titled: *"How To Write A Business Plan For Beauty Salons."* Shut the front door! I mean, really? I almost lost my lunch AND my child in that moment. I was frozen.

Instantly, I knew my purpose. I had confirmation that I was on the right track. I knew there was nothing random about me finding the book in the middle of a game of hide and seek in the cookbook section of the library. My purpose was to put this business together. I learned very early in this process that I was not alone and that my Partner (with a capital "P") would provide me with valuable tools along my journey. I picked it up and thumbed through it—everything I needed to begin my business plan was there. Meanwhile, my pissed off partner (with a little "p") stretched around the corner, arms crossed, and said: *"Momma! You quit lookin' for me."* Lord! I forgot about my child! *"I'm so sorry baby! Okay."* I stuffed the book under my arm. And our adventure began that day!

. . .

The next couple of weeks were filled with interviewing folks. The salon business plan book clarified for me what sections of information I needed. Since my dream had been about Supercuts, I started wanting a franchise. I called several salon franchises because I wanted to know how a large multi-location salon operated. Two words: Manuals and training. But I quickly realized that there were no nationally recognized Black salon chains. None. Why? The Black hair care industry is a billion-dollar industry. What's more is that during my research, I learned that while there were a few Black-owned day spas, there were no chains. That's where I got the idea to do both! Lesson Learned: Discover a need. Fill the need.

Also, I did a little cryptic, elementary marketing research, just to see what people's thoughts were about the industry. I emailed nearly 100 women from California to Virginia, from 18 years old to 68 years old, from secretaries to CEOs and asked them their thoughts about their hair salon experiences. The results? The same stuff I bitched about a few pages back! Poor timing, poor professionalism, and buying CDs! All of these things were confirmation for me. Confirming that I was on the right track.

Let's hold it right there for a minute. A Lesson Note Here: "Confirmation." What is so important about "confirmation?" When you're following a dream, it's something that you can't see. Something that doesn't exist yet. You need confirmation of certain things because it's like a bit of encouragement from the universe. It's like the universe is saying, *"Keep going! You're on the right track!"* I cannot overstate the importance of acknowledging confirmation when you are following your dreams. Because for every one piece of confirmation you receive, you will likely receive ten things that could discourage you. I put the blinders on. And looked for confirming acts so that I could stay positive during a very difficult process of accomplishing my goals. Okay, I'm done. Back to the story.

CHAPTER Six

The Perfect Name
Soul. Soul? SOUL!

Honestly, **I did not** come up with that amazingly perfect name. At the time, I was dating a wonderful guy and he actually thought of it. One night, we were at my place, and I was throwing out words, adjectives that I used to describe the business. *"I want it to be elegant, yet funky, I want music playing in the background, not elevator music or rock but old-school stuff and jazz and..."* *"How about soul?"* he said matter-of-factly. Soul? Soul. Soul! I shouted and started jumping up and down, running all around the room. He said *"Naw."* I said *"Yeah!"* And gave him an enormous smooch.

We broke up shortly thereafter. We are great friends to this day. I think he knew something I didn't... That Soul would soon be my new boo, and I was obsessed with it.

Here's an interesting point about the name and making the decision to cater to an underserved market — the Black female. It was very deliberate. It was somewhat controversial. A lot of people discouraged me, albeit subtly: "*Um...what about naming it 'Spirit,' or 'THE Soul,' or 'Body and Soul?' You want to be broad don't you?*" At the time, Soul was synonymous with Blacks and Black culture. This point was not lost upon me.

However, in 2016, Soul is very non-controversial. It is synonymous with spirit and intuition. The real reason that I love the name is that I believe we all have a soul and when you trust yours, when you follow and make soul-based decisions and not fear-based decisions, all is well. You will not go wrong. The process I was going through was a complete embodiment of that principle. Here I was an attorney who was two minutes from being unemployed thinking that I could put a business together. What made me do such a thing? My soul. And I knew that was all I needed to do. I never questioned it and that's primarily the reason that I love the name. It was perfection on every level to me. Accordingly, thanks Noah!

The soul of a business, pun intended, is truly in the details. Well, first, what did I want it to look like? I thought of myself, then, as a screenwriter. And I carefully designed each scene and character. I envisioned a place that characters on the show Girlfriends would go to. I wanted it to be elegant, yet hip and funky. I wanted earth tones—browns, golds, coppers and crèmes—for many reasons. First, I wanted it to be contemporary and comfortable and soothing. Additionally, from a branding and marketing perspective, I also wanted it to be gender neutral. I liked the concept of a man feeling comfortable coming and getting a massage or waiting patiently while his boo got her hair done.

While I was not a stylist, I had experience as a client and I knew that I always wanted wonderful customer service. I wanted the cool, gorgeous professional to support this business. In order to attract professionals, we had to be professional. We had to address the systematic problems that plague this industry. I had in my mind that from day zero, our primary policy would be "no double booking." Double booking is when you and between 2 and 10 other individuals have the same hair appointment time. This process led to a lot of angry customers in small, confined places. Again, no Bueno. If I could eliminate that in the salon, it would be a damn near revolutionary move. I didn't know if I could do it, but I was committed to that being a key component of my training and marketing strategy. Marketing and PR were also very important to me. I knew that if people saw us in magazines and stuff, it would elevate us in a real way.

To that point, I knew that I would need a beautiful website. Websites were definitely important at that time, and intuitively I knew that my peeps would need a visual. It goes without saying that I needed solid staffing policies. But my philosophy was always make it look fabulous, and everyone — team members and clients alike — will come.

CHAPTER Seven

Rent To Own

Another fun, fun, fun thing that Jason and I did in our free time? We would look for locations for the salon! Totally multitasking, right? I didn't have a relationship at the time so my focus was on point. I told him exactly what we were doing. If we were going to own a business, we needed a place. I thought U Street in Washington DC would be awesome! By way of background to those of you not familiar with DC, think of U Street like a little Harlem in New York. The street was home to the legendary Howard Theater, and many amazing musicians like Billie Holiday and Miles Davis would frequent both the theater and U Street. As with most urban neighborhoods, in the 60s, the riots had completely ravaged the area. However, by that time, the revitalization push was getting started around there. Republic Gardens — an upscale nightclub for Howard University (known affectionately as 'HU') alum, and ballers and shot callers — was on U Street. Also, Ben's Chili Bowl — where all the intoxicated students, HU alum, ballers, shot callers leaving Republic Gardens and the *Cosby Show* Bill Cosby (not the currently litigious Mr. Cosby) were known to frequent — was also on U Street. My own hair salon was on U Street. That was the place for my new business; I was sure of this fact.

In my early, ignorant days before I found Jana, I would leave work at around 5 o'clock and get my hair done across the street from *"The Gardens"* -a nightclub in DC. Then, four hours later, I would roll into *"The Gardens"* and grab the last of Chef Lois' crab cakes or jerk chicken at one of Marc Barnes' legendary extended happy hour specials. Marc Barnes was the proprietor of the Gardens, which was like a modern day Studio 54 for DC's elite urban professional. *Republic Gardens. Dream. Love. The Park.* All of these night life establishments were created for both the executive and the occasional celebrity to patronize. Without a doubt, Mr. Barnes was a major catalyst for the changes that were taking place in the area. Yes, U Street looked like the perfect place. Jason and I found a nice place right across the street that I believed would work. I took the phone number in the window down and left the owner a message expressing my interest.

I met the owner around the block about an hour later. He owned a building or two around Republic Gardens. He was a charcoal colored elderly man with slits for eyes and a knowing smirk. He let me and Jason in the building to look around. Jason took off running like a lone Jamaican bobsledder — slipping and sliding down the long narrow corridor. Nice! Spacious! I could see! Excitedly I told him about my fabulous idea about a fabulous hair salon and day spa that would work in his fabulous building. See, in retrospect, when I am enthusiastic, I talk too much. Way too much. I could see the greediness in his eyes and he could see the glee of my inexperience shooting out of my pores.

"*Well, I learned a lot about business over the years. First, if you are one month behind in your rent, I can shut you down,*" he started. O...K... My shoulders started to tense up and my jaw was tight. "*Second, I learned from my tenant, how much money I left on the table, so I get 30% of the profits of your business.*" Insert Scooby Doo face and sound here... In general, I'm not the greatest listener. I'm a visual learner. In fact, I have a photographic memory. But, when it comes to listening, I really, really have to concentrate. This problem exponentially magnifies when I'm hearing something I don't want to process, which was the case right now. In other words, the sounds coming out of the owner's mouth were now as comprehensible as Charlie Brown's teacher. Moreover, I started to visualize the robot on the old TV show, *Lost In Space* repeat over and over again in my head: "*Danger! Will Robinson! Danger!*" While the owner was still holding court, I politely nodded in agreement, did the mild version of the Electric Slide over to Jason, gently packed up my Jamaican bobsledder...and got the hell on out of there. There ain't no amount of ignorance or naivety in the world that would make me sign something like that. Some people would've thought it over. I thought: I need to own *my own* building!

CHAPTER Eight

The SBA's 504 Boyz

I don't know exactly how I first learned about the Small Business Administration's 504 program. Because I was on the phone, all the time, with all kinds of folks, I'm sure I called some bank and told them that I was opening a business and needed money. My meeting with the owner off of U Street left me frazzled about leasing, but I wasn't convinced that owning a building was an option for me. Apparently, however, it was. The SBA has a loan called the "504 loan," which allows existing and startup business owners to both purchase the property and the equipment needed to open or expand a business. How cool, right? And let me say this, I am liberal with a capital "L," but...thank you George W! The climate in the real estate market was H.O.T. and banks were giving away money like Oprah gives away cars. *"You get a bank loan! And you get a bank loan."* Within a relatively short amount of time, after hitting a few dead ends and leaving message after message, Mr. Bobby picked up the phone and returned my call.

Mr. Bobby was a friendly loan officer at the Virginia Asset Finance Corporation. He reminds me, in retrospect, of Fix-It Felix, of Wreck-It Ralph fame—just nice for no reason, nice! I remember being so excited that someone had finally given me a jingle back. Mr. Bobby explained the process of receiving money, and I believe he stated that I was required to come up with about 10% of the total price of the loan and the loan would be backed by the government, and that he would be responsible for finding a bank partner for me. All I had to do was create the business plan, which would explain what I was going to do with the money, how I was going to spend the money and how much money I was going to need.

I really didn't know anything about loans, money, financing terms. Nada. All I processed was: *"You are going to give me money to make my dream come true?" "And all I have to do is write a report? Word?"* Word. I'm on it! And just like that, I started writing.

I finished my business plan by the end of January and it was approved by February—three weeks to be exact. When I say I can write and research, I can indeed write and research. It was a throw-the-mic-down moment. I did a lot in that two months, to be sure. My credit was decent; I had a house. However, I wrote a couple of letters to creditors to take slow and late payments off and, well, they did. So my credit bumped up a bit. Cool.

. . .

Now, here's the secret about my "fantastic business plan." It was, like most startup business plans, a complete fiction, or as we say in Oakland, hella embellished. Meaning, every part of the estimate of costs were just that, estimates. They were projections. And that, mi amigo, is a major issue that most startups will have to address.

I'll give you a list of some big ticket items needed in your financial projections and startup costs. (You can skip to the next chapter if you want more drama and tension. This is where I slip into some boring yet critical financial information so proceed accordingly.) Any general business plan needs to show 1. How much it may cost to get things off the ground and 2. How you are going to make money. If you're like me, you have limited funds to pay an architect to do drawings and an engineer to do drawings, so you too will be left with estimates. Typically over the phone, general contractors will give you a dollar per square footage number. It's probably about as valuable as Peter Pan visiting you in your dreams and promising to pick up a hammer and get to work. The problem is that reality and "ballpark" figures can be as far away as Earth is to the newly non-existing planet of Pluto. And this is a big red flag for many reasons, the least of which is that you may not have enough money to finish your dream. Aside from construction and architecture costs, other items such as equipment and supplies are clearer to measure.

The challenge is that you have to think of everything from music, to towels, to rollers. That is yet another reason that a business blueprint or roadmap plan is so important. It forces you to research every single detail and anticipate everything and the more detailed you are, the better. With that being said, for as detailed as my plan was, I still had highly insane surprises and expenses that I had to deal with. But the better organized you are with your plan, the more ammunition you have to address the unexpected.

So let's stick with what made my business plan accepted in three weeks! Well, the most important thing was that the political, economic and real estate climates were all outstanding. Banks were lending, and I had good credit and I was trying to purchase property. While I would love to take credit and say that my outstanding literary prose was the singular reason for my loan approval, I think that it was the opposite. It was timing.

At the end of the day, I received two loans: a 504 loan and a 7a startup capital loan. I think my 7a loan was for $70,000 and my 504 loan was for $400,000. What I didn't have was a piece of property to purchase, an architect or a contractor. I also had a crazy unrealistic timeframe. Remember, I would be unemployed in about four minutes?? Everything was just exciting and aggressive and adrenaline inducing. I didn't have any active addictions that I was aware of, but this shit was my obsession, for real! I loved every moment of it.

CHAPTER Nine

My Architect She-Ro!

What came first? Selecting a fabulous architect. Washington DC is a fabulous city for resources such as trade associations, embassies and government agencies. I would spend hours in Borders and Barnes & Noble with my son. We'd sit quietly in the children's section on the floor where he'd have his snack and stack of Barney, Batman and Teletubbies books and mommy would have 20 interior design magazines. Stacks on stacks on stacks. Hours and hours. Fabulous fun for all. And it was through those magazines that I realized that the American Institute of Architects (AIA) was right down the street from my gig.

As an aside, I was always a mommapreneur before the term was officially a "thing." I took Jason everywhere with me and explained appropriately what we were doing. When I looked at a site, he was with me and I got his input. Wall color selection? I let him test paint with me. Interviewed an architect? He sat quietly with a coloring book and bananas and snacks. Always present. Always asking. Always understanding.

Back to the AIA. I visited the AIA. The AIA had portfolios of architects who worked locally. I quickly narrowed my choices down to two immensely talented architects. While I went on two "dates," I was blown away by bachelorette number two — Ms. Emma Greenberg of *Greenberg Design Studio*. I remember our first meeting was at *Polly's Café*, a little neighborhood dive, based on her recommendation. Polly's was a risk-taking venture on U Street, one of the early trailblazers that knew something new and exciting was coming to the city, and it was making its first stop on the U Street corridor. The restaurant was tucked in the basement level of a row house so the only light in the room came from the enthusiastic brilliance of Emma's eyes when she popped through the door. I could not tell which element of her face sparkled more brightly — her teeth or her eyes! I loved her immediately.

She was about 5'2, a petite little woman with chestnut brown hair. She was a wisp of a woman, but her firm handshake did not get THAT memo. It was powerful. It conveyed to me that she was comfortable with being the only chick on a construction site or something. I stood up to greet her and my 5'9 frame and shadow nearly eclipsed her. But in terms of energy and congeniality, we were equally matched.

Selecting great people is my strong suit, me thinks, and Emma was smart, hungry, hard-working and pleasant. Oh and reasonably priced. A creative who was flexible and humble. Humility is a character trait that people undervalue. The ability to say *"Hey, I don't understand,"* or *"I completely screwed this up"* is worth a great deal. Emma brought her portfolio and letters of recommendation from previous customers. She gave me a budget on hours and a schedule for how my project would proceed and told me how involved I could ever want to be. She had limited retail or commercial experience, but was willing to learn and was really interested in doing a day spa so we agreed to do the construction/design dance. So now that I had a fabulous architect on board, there was just a tiny detail that needed to be addressed... A location!

CHAPTER Ten

Location...Location...LOCATION.

OK, here's the thing: This is the benefit of hindsight, and I can be truthful. I really wanted to be on U Street, but I put bids on a few locations and did not get any of them. When my real estate agent, Mr. Noah, said, *"Have you considered looking further down past U Street, to Florida Avenue?"* I was clueless that anything even existed *"down there."* Seriously, that should've been a yellow/red flag. When Mr. Noah provided me with the address and asked me to meet him at the three level row house at 25 Florida Avenue, NW, I did. As I slowly drove to the end of the earth of the street known as the 0 block of Florida Avenue, Northwest, several thoughts shot through my brain. First thought: It is SHAD-Y around here. Unlike U Street, the only "retail" spaces within a three block radius were a low-priced gas station, three liquor stores and a Chinese carryout. And the "pedestrian traffic" consisted of only those brave souls who were scurrying to and from the bus stop. I thought to myself: This is a problem, Shorty (my DC speak).

I sat in my car, all "inconspicuous" in my Mercedes Benz CLK320, completely spooked out. I looked at the bus stop at the intersection of Florida and North Capitol Street. There were about five older brothas in the center of the bus stop island, "holding court" on crates and "joning on" any and every person with the fortitude to pass them. *"Shaw-tay! You ain't missing no happy meals, are you?"* Laughter erupts. The female pedestrian kindly greets them all with the middle finger salute without missing a beat. I cringed. Two ambulances with their piercingly and painfully loud sirens then passed by in rapid succession—another red flag. What was I thinking? Spas equal elegance and class and bougie-ness and this place ain't it!

Were there ANY green flags? Well, next to the building was an open vacant, private lot that used to be an Exxon gas station. I pondered. Maybe I could secure a deal with the owner and have my customers park there. Maybe. Maybe Not. Well, by now all of these neon red flags were flashing, like when you come to a four-way signal, at 2 AM, and each one is blinking brightly...and simultaneously. Exact...Slow...and perfectly timed. Yeah, a moment like that. Well, hell, let me not be judgmental, I nervously thought. I soon saw Mr. Noah pull up and park behind my ride.

I got out, and quickly locked my car. Mr. Noah smiled his nicely groomed real estate smile, and I in turn shot him my sista girl side eye, which said: *"Mr. Noah, are you serious? This area is...in transition...*" I mentally clutched my pearls! Sensing my reluctance, he quickly stated, "*Nicole, this area is up-and-coming. Before you make a decision, let's go inside.*"

As my young professional Nine West pumps click clacked across Florida Avenue, I was so sure that this was... Not the business. However, I was up against mind-numbing details and deadlines... My friendly neighborhood law firm was about to play my *"dead man walking"* theme music, which left me with a tiny window to get this thing off the ground. Or maybe the neighborhood would receive some gentrification love on this block? Even my inner devil's advocate chuckled— she didn't believe it her damn self. She couldn't even finish the sentence without a little condemnation. Her sarcastic ass.

25 Florida was objectively an attractive building on the outside. There were two stories and a basement and while it was officially an end row house, it was very spacious. As I would later see on the blueprint, for all my geometry geeks, it was a "tangential trapezoid" — meaning it was a cross between a triangle and a square — much more spacious than your average row house.

Okay, so we unlocked the padlock on the door i.e. a wooden slab with the chain and lock on it. We walked over the threshold and I felt like I had stepped into the role of an extra on the set of *Jungle Fever* minus the smoke... Remember where Gator and Halle Berry *"were smoking mama's TV."* For those who didn't get the reference... I stepped into an abandoned crack house! I.

Was. Horrified. It was dark and cold. There was no electricity in there — the only way we could see anything was from the sunlight peeking in from newly installed windows. And while I was no CSI expert, I could deduce that there was drug looking stuff — i.e. used matches, lighters, tin foils, and ashes — on the premises. Say it with me now: SHAD-Y.

Mr. Noah was speechless. I was about to spin around and let Mr. Noah fend for himself, but his pleading eyes and voice said let's take a look upstairs. Jiminy Crickets! I looked to the right, where a staircase should have been and in its place was a make shift ladder. Where's the elevator, man, I thought, completely frazzled by now. Dude, surely you don't expect me to physically climb up this Lego Land engineered ladder? Well... I had my man was blushing and sweating at the same time. Good grief. I started to ascend up into the drug infested loft like a *New Jack City* extra at the Carter.

If climbing the ladder wasn't bad enough, I'm deathly afraid of heights. When I got to the midway point, chile, I made the mistake of looking down. Surprise! There was no floor underneath. I literally could see all the way down into the basement. Jesus take the wheel! I paused for composure. Then I did what I do, I pushed past the fear and raced to the top safely.

When I got to the top, I turned the corner and was in complete and utter shock at what I saw. It was breathtaking! Twenty foot high ceilings! A clean open floor plan. And the windows! There was a wall full of windows that let the sunshine right in. Immediately, I could envision how gorgeous it would be.

I could see ceiling to floor curtains covering the window panes. I could see the stylist stations and envision the ladies laughing and drinking their tea and others sitting under the dryers working on their briefs from work or thumbing through the latest issue of Cosmo or ESSENCE magazine. I also could imagine this beautiful space being rented out for a VIP reception or a client appreciation day. I could hear the O'Jays or Beyoncé playing softly while the authentic smell of pressed hair lingered in the background... I no longer saw this empty shell in its current state. I saw it for what it could be—a gorgeous, urban oasis for women and men to retreat from their worries and pains and hurts. If only for a couple of hours.

I envisioned a quality and ethical work environment for women who wanted a better life for themselves and their families. I knew the existing salons were typically filled with headaches and chaos—I envisioned a sweeter reality, however. One that I could control and spearhead. I knew my heart. I knew my intention. I knew my purpose. I wanted a place for women to feel a sense of pride and love. I wanted Soul Day Spa and Salon to embody my intention and purpose. I turned to my realtor, who looked at me hopefully. *"Write up a contract Mr. Noah. Let's do this!"*

CHAPTER Eleven

"Who Put This Thing Together??"
–Al Pacino in Scarface

The construction process was exciting! Thrilling! Hellacious! Every adjective you know — just throw them all out because at some point, I experienced every one of them. I got a few coins from the bank to do architectural drawings and engineer drawings. Those were completed by Emma and her boy, the engineering dude. Engineering dude was tight — he did an excellent job and was reasonably priced. And Emma had a contractor that she was so confident in. She had worked with him in the past, and she was absolutely certain that he could do the job for our price. And anxious Annie, i.e. me, excitedly assumed that it was all good. Remember, we only had a few months to get this done before the bank required me to start paying them on the notes. While Emma and engineer dude were working feverishly to complete the blueprints, I turned my attention to the 4,700 other things on the list that needed to get done.

I did stop for one moment and say, *"OMFG! I know nothing about the day spa industry!!"* And guess what? That goes for the hair industry too. Oh, and that's right — I've never operated a friggin' business before either!! I needed some basic understanding of...everything! So I started researching the licensing aspects of this biz. First, there were four licenses involved: Cosmetology? Two years to complete. Nope-too long. Nail tech? Not touching anybody's feet that older than three years old...Nope-Nope. Massage therapist? NAKEDness — Yikes! Nope. Finally, Aesthetics? Sounds good. Faces are fine. I used evenings and weekends to take the course and research the industry on which I was betting the farm.

Okay, I know I'm wrong, but when it comes to education, I'm pretty elitist. I also believe you get what you pay for. This "school spa" I attended was the worst. First, the owner was a pimp. I mean, she had a school in the back and the spa was in the front and she would "train" the students who had taken about two days of classes and then she would set us free on to unsuspecting clients and not compensate us. All legal. I mean, most places wait at least four minutes before they let students loose. Anyway, I'm a good student, so I did my time and got the hell up out of there.

Next, I also joined an amazing trade association. *The Professional Beauty Association*, formerly known as *The Salon Association*, was a wealth of information. The organization was devoted to uplifting the image of the industry and being a mentor for new and existing members. They provided employee manuals, marketing information, product knowledge and education to its members. I cannot overstate what an important part of this process it was for me.

For one, the leaders in the industry were very knowledgeable, yet giving and generous individuals. They truly, truly had a love for the industry and really wanted the world to respect it. They also wanted owners to have pride in their businesses. Everything I learned about operating a spa/salon business and how to train employees and how to market and advertise a business was instilled in me by *The Salon Association*. The funny thing is that I was a member before I opened and probably for the first couple of years that I was running the business. One of the most valuable things I got from the association was an introduction to a darling woman by the name of Olivia Lander who was on the board at that time.

She was a beautiful cinnamon colored woman from Cleveland, Ohio with a salon called Le Blanc. I simply called her on the phone one day and told her I needed a mentor. She was the only woman of color on the board and, honestly, I was hopeful that she would extend some assistance to me as a newbie. We had a lovely conversation and she was a wealth of information, even in that short period of time. She told me that if I could get out to Ohio, she would tell me everything I needed to know. She and her husband were very kind and opened their home to me. I went to visit her salon. I saw the salon software that the front desk used. I saw how many phone lines she had. I saw what was at each station in terms of product lines and the colors that were used. I saw that all her stylists wore uniforms. I saw how she paid her staff based on commission rates, not booth rent like I saw a lot in DC. She and her husband advised me against having a day spa too; however, I struggled with that advice. I didn't just want a salon. My vision from the beginning included the entire package. So I listened, and kept it moving.

Stepping out of narrative format, this was a critical step in opening a business—networking with those who do what you are doing or want to do. You are going to learn from the leaders. The leaders have already made the mistakes that you are going to make. They allow you to build on their successes and avoid their failures. They are givers, not takers. They have learned that true success occurs through being of service to others. They are not greedy. They typically are humble and know the value of information is not to keep it a secret. It is for the world. It is one of the central reasons for writing this book.

With regard to other training I received, I used some of the startup funds to attend a salon management incubator. I believe this was extremely helpful. It was based in Arizona, and I went with a friend who I, at the time, believed was going to assist in managing the salon. There were several other owners who participated as well. The most important take away from that seminar? I learned how to read financial projections on Excel spreadsheets for salons. Priceless. It showed me the estimates for revenue and expenses for a small salon. One of the principles of management I also learned was that I should be a "no commission" salon. Their most important management principle was that salary should be tied to performance. In fact, they had an elaborate chart that had tiers of performance from entry level to management. I really understood the logic behind it. It gave people financial goals that were tied to productivity and other things like professionalism, attendance, chores and referrals. In theory, this was an effective thoughtful way of conducting a business. In sum, the esthetician course, trade association mentors and salon incubators were how I gained valuable industry/management lessons on what I would do once I opened the business.

. . .

While I was spending half of my time learning about the industry, I felt like I should be taking heart meds to deal with the daily stress of the construction process. Because I was limited on money, I did not hire Emma as the construction project manager. I hired the most qualified person for my price point — Me. For no money. Actually this was not a fatal mistake, although the construction process was filled with peaks and valleys and lots of on-the-job training.

For my friends who have never gone through the construction process, consider yourself blessed — I'm sure you have extended your lifespan. In short, once your drawings for your space are done, you have to "bid" the job out to see what a contractor will charge you to build the thing. Thus in my case, once Emma finished the blueprints, we had to shop around and price it. Well, Emma had a company in mind that she was so certain would be able to do the job for our minuscule budget. So she calls me and asks, can we meet to discuss the price her contractor friend gave her. We met at a *Cosi* restaurant on Connecticut Avenue in the Northwest section of DC. Emma was early. I spotted her though she was nearly unrecognizable — her signature smile and positive energy had politely excused themselves from the table and gone to the restroom or something. I really grew concerned. Her face was sullen and her enthusiasm was MIA. *"What's wrong?"* I said. *"I don't know how to say this so I'm just going to,"* Emma said directly. My heart exited my body and joined her enthusiasm in another room. *"The contractor came in three times higher than our budget. In essence, we would only be able to complete about two of the three floors. Nicole, I don't know what happened. I'm so sorry!"* My home girl kept it together, but I could tell she was mortified.

I was pissed. I hadn't even sat down yet. Why did she bring me to Cosi to tell me this? She should have set the mood right and taken me to a damn bar. *"What the hell happened, Emma?"* She started to rattle off facts and numbers and requirements and it was like she had morphed into the *Peanuts* gang's teacher. Wah, Wah. Wah. I couldn't take it anymore. Wait. Stop. *"Are you saying he the only one we requested a bid from?"* *"Yes,"* she said kind of matter-of-factly. *"Why is that?"* I said with my attitude in high gear. I was always the *"nice girl."* It was a genetic set of characteristics passed down from my nice and pleasant Grandma Watson. We really didn't DO angry very well, especially in public. But, yes, in that moment, I could (and did) pull out my sista girl authority voice on those rare occasions when I needed to get my point across. Unfortunately, for Emma, this was such an occasion.

I really relied heavily on Emma in this area. She was relatively new, but experienced and she was so excited and confident that this guy would work. I'm a sucker for passion and enthusiasm. At this time, I was very new to the game of business. My gut is a skeptic, but my heart wears bright pink shades of optimism and my mind is a focused and patient Indy 500 NASCAR driver. They all fit like a little dysfunctional family. Right now, Gut, was speaking. *"Emma, I need you to find me more contractors to bid on this project. One monkey will not stop this show. This is going to work and I'm not worried. (Lie.) I'm confident that you will find another team. (Bigger lie. There's a thin line between denial and motivation.) You can do it. Now. Do they serve alcohol here?"*

I looked very confident. I didn't yell, yet I was internally hyperventilating. But whatever I said and however I said it, I got my point across very clearly. Emma's moment of defeat was waning. *"Well, I know a few companies, one is based out of Maryland, and I also checked with my previous boss for references."* Emma was back in the saddle. They had no liquor or white zinfandel, so I settled for a shot of espresso. It worked just fine.

. . .

What were the major construction problems? Number one: The plumbing. The pipeline that carried the water from the street was too small. Number two: The water heater. We needed a commercial sized one. Number three: The sprinkler situation. The HVAC system. And one huge problem was a basement that was under sea level. In short, construction was a bloody (in the English jargon) water nightmare. Leo and *The Titanic* had nothing on us. Water was coming from everywhere except where we needed it to flow.

Did I mention that 25 Florida Ave. was underwater? Not literally, but every time it rained, water will come from somewhere. So the entire construction project was plagued by new issues surrounding water and here's the thing, none of these issues were contemplated in the original blueprint. How could they be? It's one of those things that comes along with risk-taking territory. I soon found out that I was built for this stuff. My mantra was 'it will get done.' I just didn't know how. Tim Gunn of *Project Runway* would later coin the wonderful phrase that all entrepreneurs instinctive live by: *"Make It Work."* And I personally love the phrase: *"Keep It Moving."*

Jacob Gran was the new contractor that Emma found, and if 25 Florida was an underwater vessel, Jacob was our *Aquaman*. He was so pleasant, even on the worst days. He gave me options to resolve the problems, all of which were followed by phrases like *"this is the least expensive solution"* or *"this is the only option we have,*

Nicole." I got my on-the-job construction manager training, and Jacob and his crew labored away at building Soul.

CHAPTER Twelve

Designer Diva Denise

I think you have a pretty clear understanding of how Soul was constructed. The only part I forgot was how the beautiful interior space was developed, which was definitely the single most important part of my strategy to making this work in an area that was...sketchy. A couple of people and companies were instrumental in that process. First, Richard Silver was with Belvedere, a salon furnishings company. He was so helpful in talking me through my look and hopes for the space. I found him by looking at trade magazines like Salon Today and Day Spa Magazine. Takara Belmont and Belvedere were consistently named as the leaders in the salon and spa industry for furnishings. Richard was the only one on my team who really understood industry specific things like, how many shampoo bowls will fit in a particular space and how much walking space a stylist would need around them or what type of lighting is needed to fill a space or how functional some styling stations are versus others. The list was specific and very long. He also helped me get... The Vichy Shower.

The idea for Soul being housed in a renovated home and the Vichy Shower were inspired by... The *Sugarhouse Day Spa and Salon* in Old Town, Alexandria, Virginia. I went there while I was still practicing law. And that was my first experience with The Vichy Shower. I was a Vichy Shower virgin because it was life changing for me. Let me explain...The Vichy Shower. Think of a shower big enough to fit a bed in and imagine yourself laying down on that said bed. Now, envision six shower heads coming from the ceiling and positioned over your feet, your back and your shoulders. Sound nice, huh? Well that is what the Vichy Shower is. And it was the leading lady in my Soul cast. I always envisioned that this spa service would set us apart from our competition. Spas typically have the following features: massage, skin services, body treatments i.e. shower saunas etc. nail services, and waxing. But not everyone has a Vichy Shower. I wanted that from day one. I thought it was a wonderful experience that many people did not know about. I wanted to introduce folks to it.

As I envisioned it in my business plan, I wanted Soul to be gender-neutral — neutral colors and I wanted it to be "ethnic chic," meaning I wanted interesting artwork from cultures around the world. I wanted a minimalist theme of darkened mahogany floors, light and airy wall colors and chocolate accents. I described myself as an elegantly laid-back woman. I never wanted to appear pretentious. I wanted my business to read back that authenticity. In order to achieve the look that was so clear in my head, I would need an accomplice. A fabulous one. She came in a pretty, elegant package named Denise Mills. I honestly can't remember how we met. Okay, I just cheated and asked her. She said we met at a Christmas party and she said that she and I hit it off immediately. This is true—she is hilarious! She wore glasses and a little cropped Afro and she always looked over the top of her glasses like you were a fine specimen of artwork in her classroom. She was refined and knowledgeable about all things furniture. But this culture diva had a laser tongue of wit.

I told her that I was putting together a spa, and she was intrigued. She offered to assist me with the design of the interior in exchange for the experience. Sounded good to my ignorant ass. I know what I know, and I know what I don't know. I didn't know that you can kill otherwise fabulous relationships off of agreements like that. But, we were both very green in our industries. In retrospect, we spent hundreds! (no hyperbole) of hours playing with wall coloring and floor samples and beautifully designed chairs and commercial graded fabrics and foot basins for pedicures and on and on and on.

Then after about the 950th hour of fun, Denise raised the point of compensation. I was utterly embarrassed. I thought we were friends... *"But you said..."* She was absolutely right... But we should have, in retrospect, limited the hours, put it in writing, and thought of a reasonable amount that I could afford. I also could have agreed to mention her in all publications that discuss design. But we didn't. I think she said she never got any clients as a result. That makes me genuinely sad.

. . .

True Denise story: I remember that I wanted matchy-matchy dark stations and dark floors and light walls. Denise, the artist, was terrified that it would be boring. In fact, I remember the wall, color sample day. Jason, aged 5, assisted when we were choosing between two creamy colors. One was a golden cream and one was kind of a malty cream. I believe we selected the golden cream. Anyhoo, it was installation day. I was so excited. Denise was going to meet me at the site. The colors were now up, and the styling stations were being installed. It would all be together for my excited little eyes to see! Yay! I was running over small children and the elderly (hyperbole) to get there when Denise calls. I smiled as I picked up the phone. *"Girl, how does everything look???"* She was literally crying on the phone. *"Girl, it's awful!"*

"Awful?" I was so confused. How can cream and brown be awful—they are neutrals, girlfriend...? She was really against my matchy-matchy, monochromatic color palette. But, I was very clear about what feeling I wanted. I know that Denise wanted a funky, eclectic vibe, but I discovered how much I loved interior design through this process. I also learned that I'm a creature with an exceptional eye for color and evoking a mood through balance and texture.

After verbally resuscitating Denise on the phone, I pulled up to the building, screeched to a stop, ran across the street, and knocked over a few construction workers traveling down the stairs as I raced up past them to the top of the stairs. I got to the top of the stairs and saw a miracle in front of me. It was my vision come to life! We did it! Even if Denise was wet in the face with disappointment, my feeling of elation was obviously very different than her reaction. And I assured her that I loved it, and I would take full responsibility if people in the public were as teary face as she was. I think the strain of the process was wearing down on her a bit, but I was elated.

There is nothing that can explain the feeling of seeing something dreamed about for so long come to life. Maybe that was the reason that the baby analogy seems so trite, yet effective. You spend forty weeks of your life thinking, praying, and obsessing over the little life growing inside of you, daydreaming about the perfect name. What will she look like? Will she look the same as you envisioned her to be? When I turned that corner I realized that I had given birth to something beautiful. Giving birth is one thing. Raising a child is another.

. . .

While construction may seem like a technical topic, the experience was extremely drama filled for me. It also taught me a few hard-earned lessons about business ownership. The first is, you would think having a checkbook from the bank would translate to people lining up at the door to do the project. Nope. Here is the way the process typically happens. You have money advanced to do the architecture drawings and then you get companies to bid on the project. The challenge is that the bank approves a loan that is purely speculative. I put a bid on a property without knowing if I would have enough money to do everything necessary to create a day spa and salon. Had the process gone the textbook way, the owner or potential owner would know where all the bodies are buried. I mean, an appraisal is one thing, but it does not determine whether the use you want is practical or viable. As one can imagine—except naïve Nicole (that's me), there are ten thousand specific things that go into putting a day spa together particularly into a 1906... abandoned house. I know you are not supposed to assume, but I didn't know anything about banking or financing a 504 loan. Call me crazy, but I did assume that the bank had thought their process through and it would work.

There were several major problems that resulted from the way this deal was structured. One would prove to be fatal for the business in the long run. First, as I mentioned, I received two loans: one was for construction and one was for startup capital. Sounds good right? Well the major problem is that I had to start repaying the loan before construction was completed. Also, timewise, I literally had not closed on the property for two minutes before we were rushing up against that damned bank's clock. And another little tickler... We went to closing on 25 Florida ONE week before my swan song was playing at the law firm.

CHAPTER Thirteen

St. Stephen's and Lil' Ruby Bridges

While all this construction and design drama was going on, I was still working my 9 to 5 at the law firm. Remember—they gave me exactly six months to get my shit together, i.e. find another gig. Well, in that six months, I had been quite the busy bee—I created a business plan; got that business plan approved; selected an architect/construction/design team AND selected a site. What I had not done yet was find interim employment during the construction phase. And, as of June 2002, I was going to be out of work at my "high powered" lawyer gig. In fact, my colleagues were planning a big going away party for me. I told them I was going to be an entrepreneur and that I was opening an upscale day spa. What I didn't share with them was that I had just closed on the property, which meant I was a week from having two mortgages, and hernia (literally,) and no income.

As I sat in my office thinking about how my "perfectly" planned idea was not so perfectly prepared or timed for this day, I carefully stood up from my mahogany desk, gently closed my office door and had a complete and graphic panic attack. I had been moving so fast in faith, dealing with architects and banks that I never completely thought this part through. How would I live during construction and while the business was getting off the ground?

The cry that erupted from my body was so violent it scared me, and I had to remember the steps and processes for breathing. One, you inhale through your nose, and two, you exhale through your mouth and three, repeat this process until you calm your high yellow ass down! The process worked for a minute, but then I could feel another natural disaster arising from within me. This one felt more like a torrential rain or tsunami or anything that included water—lots and lots of water in the northern hemisphere of my face. I cannot do this here! Everyone thinks I'm happy. Little Miss Entrepreneur in training. Get. It. Together. Get it together?! We don't have a job! WE don't have money to pay for your two mortgages, your child, your bills, and your ass goes out and thinks it's a great idea to give up a $145,000 a year job to start... A beauty shop?! Ms. Hard-Core Truth was bitter and not compassionate in this moment. She was not a fan of my strategy. Let's take a little walk please—Miss Compassion had my back. Find sunglasses. Find keys. Smile. Open the door and walk.

I remember walking out of the building and being determined, committed to not crying until I found a safe place so that meant I had to walk down the street like a cross between a panicked mom looking for a misplaced child and a substance abuser. My head and neck and eyes searched frantically, left, right, left, right. *Subway* sandwich? Nope. *Domino's*? Nope. My staccato steps were stuttered, haphazard and uncertain. I kept walking in a daze until suddenly my cloudy vision cleared, and parted like the Red Sea when I looked across the street and saw a Catholic Church. That was it! I ran across the busy intersection like an old-school Frogger videogame character, a little winded, but unharmed. The sensation in my hand returned just long enough to reach for the church front door and... It was closed. What? The... I can't cuss, right? This is awful.

I ran to the side where there was a little courtyard and a gatekeeper was picking up trash. With an intense smile, I bum rushed him. Is there another door open? I might as well have started scratching up my arms at the time like an addict. He didn't look up from his project and pointed to the end of the courtyard. And so I ran, down to the center of the church to the side of the center most pew. The enormity of the uncertainty of my life crashed down forcefully on me. I wept uncontrollably. God and me. Me and God. He was quiet. I was loud. What am I doing? Did you really want me to do this? This way? Did I misread a cue or something? I mean, maybe I just thought you wanted me to do this. I was spiraling by now. After a few more rants, I could see that second-guessing myself was getting me nowhere.

It was a very unilateral conversation, really. So I stopped. I was all cried out. I shut down my mind to the random, frightened angry second-guessing thoughts and focused on repeating one phrase. Help me. Help me. Help me. I do remember that my walk back to work that last day was calm and purposeful.

When I got back to the office, I was greeted with a beautiful goodbye party that was really well attended. The cake even had a picture of a blow dryer and scissors and nail polish! My friend and work husband, Mason, a 6 foot 11 former basketball player turned poet turned attorney, quietly assisted me in packing up my office. He removed my black and white Billie Holiday poster from my wall, as well as the infamous Norman Rockwell painting reprinted titled, *"The Problem We All Live With."* It was a bold choice, I thought, to put it up. It was a picture of little Ruby Bridges walking to school, you know, in her cotton white dress, socks and matching ribbon in her hair. She was a brave little girl who was one of the first Blacks to integrate schools in the South. To put it mildly, she was not well received. In this print, she was boxed perfectly in the center of four U.S. marshals protecting her steps. While in the back of her was faintly printed the word "nigger." I paused.

Here I was, a few generations later, a well-educated, well respected and well treated, woman embarking on something unconventional, but it was good. It felt good. What was I afraid of really? I looked back at my girl, lil' Ruby. I looked at the erectness of her back — she was not shaking. She did not even have her parents there to hold her hand. She held her head up high.

I was taking a risk. I really had no idea of exactly how this entire thing was going to turn out. Little Ruby had a great deal of uncertainty in front of her. Her delicate six-year-old frame was possibly in jeopardy. But she held onto her book and just kept walking. In the great scheme of things, my journey was far less... Important. Obviously, I would have to find employment during the construction phase. Surely I could do that, right? I had a little money stashed under my pillow for days like this. A shift in perspective was always a mental game changer for me. And most importantly, I had asked God, in my most pitiful way, I knew, for help. The two of us always worked very well together, and I'm sure that Little Ruby's parents instilled in her the power of God. It was evident in her walk and in her face. The same God that protected her was surely guiding me now, right? I took a deep breath. We finished packing the last of my things, I held my head up a bit higher, walked a little taller and headed out my office for the last time.

It didn't take long for that prayer to be answered. When I got home I had received a message from a law firm wanting to schedule an interview with me for an administrative position with them. That was just what I needed to make ends meet until Soul was born.

PART Two
ESTABLISH.

CHAPTER Fourteen

Operations...In the Beginning

I've taken you through several very important stages of the entrepreneurial process: First, you have to have a viable concept, a business plan and finances. Then, if you are doing a storefront, you will obviously go through the construction and design phase. Finally, you open and operate. And my silly ass thought the hardest part was behind me. Seriously...I did.

From 2003 to the end of 2009, I operated the business and expanded to a second location and closed both of them. Personally, during that same time frame, I reconnected with an old boyfriend, got a new house, got married, had a baby and got a divorce. To say the least, I did a hell of a lot of living during that time period. This next section of the book attempts to accomplish a few things. First, in order to operate a business, your marketing, financial management, and employee management skills need to be firing on all cylinders on a regular basis. I will highlight some of the major things that happened in those areas and how I built and sustained Soul during those years. But obviously, there were some major setbacks along the way as well. I'll share them too. Finally, I'll show you what happened when I was going home after Soul. This way, you will see the highlights and lowlights in my work/life imbalance.

. . .

I opened Soul in the middle of June 2003, after nearly a year of construction—about seven months longer than we anticipated. As difficult as it was to get the doors open, it was even more challenging to keep them open. And while I considered myself a damn good business plan writer, I didn't know the first thing about actually operating a business. A lot of my management and business acumen was on-the-job, fly-by-the-seat-of-my-pants learning, reacting and planning after a screw up. I developed a Keep It Simple Stupid method of business growth. I needed money. In order to get money, I needed customers. In order to get customers, I needed team members and a good name.

The first few months in business were so difficult. Nothing was instinctive. The building itself had so many reoccurring problems. The huge water heater needed time to warm up...what? That thing was huge and brand new, so when we started using it for everything including the Vichy Shower, we had episodes when the water would go ice cold for a few moments. And speaking of the Vichy Shower, that monstrosity also had to be broken in. As I shared earlier, a Vichy Shower is an amazing six showerhead shower that we used when we did body wraps and salt scrubs. The client would lay down on a water proof bed, then the esthetician would apply the treatment and finally, the six shower heads would run water over the client's shoulders, back and legs to experience...heaven. As you can imagine, in the beginning, there was a learning curve. The room had a drain and was waterproofed with ceramic tile, which was beautiful. But sometimes, the technician would accidentally cover the drain and the downstairs would have water all over. The carpet right outside the room would be soaked.

Another challenge? Rain, waterproofing, roofs and sump pumps. I didn't know until it was too late, but that building was in an area in DC that Noah and his crew would have found troubling to navigate. Every TIME it rained and I mean every time, water would stealthily gain access into my building like the crew in Ocean's Eleven, Twelve and Thirteen. Water would trickle into the bathroom windows, the floor, the roof and the door, at times simultaneously. And the repairs were not an inexpensive solution. I was broke for nearly the entire duration of Soul and things like sump pumps, roofs and new windows were summarily denied by my pocketbook and bank account.

Other challenges? Employment issues were tough in the beginning. Within the first year, we had high turnover. Also, another huge issue was that in the District of Columbia, every salon needed a manager with a manager's cosmetology license on site. Makes sense. This was where my lack of being a cosmetologist hurt me initially. I had to rely on other people to keep my business operating. The manager's license created problems for me on a couple of fronts. If the person with the manager's license received too many complaints, I had to hurry and replace them, which left me vulnerable of operating without a license. I know you are asking, why didn't you just get a cosmetology license? That was never a realistic option. It would take too much time and money, both of which were in very limited supply at that point.

That was a situation that kept me up late at night, every night, when I opened. While I could make the place look fabulous, if a stylist turned a customer's hair green (which happened), I had no acumen to remedy the situation. Also, relying on another person for my business created a needy relationship with, at times, unreliable or untalented folks. That was so stressful. Finally, I had to rely on the stylists and the spa staff to manage themselves. If customers complained one time too many in the early days, I let the team members go. I knew that if we received too many complaints too early in the process, it would kill our brand.

Speaking of brands, I knew that as soon as I opened my doors, I had to get clients in there and keep them happy. That was my singular goal. Our brand was simple: *"Nothing is more important than the time, appearance and feelings of our guests."* I always approached Soul as if someone were coming to my home as my guest. I really enjoy entertaining and being a host.

I always wanted to make people feel good. So my business was a natural extension of my personality.

Time. Appearance. Feelings. While I did not have experience as a stylist, I had years of experience as a customer, remember? Now I could, I theorized, right all the wrongs of the salon industry. The bottom line was that I really worked hard to create a professional environment. Professionalism for me was a straight forward, non-compromising principal. Professionalism meant being on-time. Professionalism meant being pleasant to everyone who was gracious enough to pay us money and support us. Professionalism meant looking like a wonderful representation of the service you are providing. Hell, to me, professionalism meant wearing uniforms of all black. And last but not least, professionalism meant providing a technically proficient service. I never got overly intimidated by what I didn't know how to do. I hired the best and held them accountable. I let them know my expectations early and often and then I let them fly. And slowly but surely, the team started to come together, and the guests followed soon after.

It's difficult to distill eight years of business into a few operational anecdotes, but I'll try. Again, marketing, management and money are the key responsibilities that I had, that all business owners have. Take a peek at some of the issues I had in those areas.

CHAPTER Fifteen

Marketing Your Soul

Looking back, I don't think that I had a real strategic plan on how to attract people to Soul. But I had a general idea: I need to be in the magazines. That was the goal. When we opened, we had a little buzz going for us, but not much. Remember, this was 2003, and social media as we know it was not born yet. Literally. Facebook began one year later. That is so amazing to me now. I really had to do a grassroots campaign to get Soul off the ground. I used my email database of friends. My girlfriends, actually. They were my target market. And I just built from there.

The truth is, I only had about seven girlfriends, so I needed to broaden the base, to say the least. And fast. First, I put together a media kit. I had a great graphic designer named Jeremy Wood. He had an amazing eye and created all the visuals for the business over its eight years of existence. My press kit was basically a few of our cards, a little press release about how I got started, and most importantly, pictures of the salon.

As I mentioned earlier, I was gambling a lot on the decor and the design. If it didn't look good, not one woman would come to the ghetto to even step foot in the place. To work or to get a service. I invested a few dollars in a professional photographer to come and take pictures of the most visually appealing spots in the space. And then I literally looked at every magazine that I thought my potential clients would read, found the editors, found the addresses, and sent press kits to them all. *Sophisticates Black Hair* was the first to respond. I found out quickly that being new and being cute were newsworthy events. They were the first magazine that we were featured in. I was thrilled and felt that we were gaining some traction, but the sales and customers were still trickling in. I didn't know what to do.

I had always dreamed about being featured in *ESSENCE* magazine. I had sent several press kits to the editors but we got no hits. I remember one Saturday, I was working late at the salon. I read somewhere that Kevin Powell was in town signing his new book at Howard University's bookstore. It was right down the street from Soul, and I had always admired Kevin. By way of background, Kevin Powell was one of the original cast members of the MTV show, *The Real World*. Yes, I had a slight crush on him when I was a teenager. But over the years he had beefed up his resume by becoming a music editor for *Vibe* magazine and had gone on to be a hip-hop critic, author, political commentator and activist. He was good friends with one of my high school buddies. As I was sweeping up and closing out the register for the day, I thought maybe I would go by and just check him out and support him on his book tour.

I put on a skirt with my white work blouse and drove down the street to Howard University. I purchased a book and introduced myself to him, saying, *"Hey, I'm a friend of Scott Gordon's."* He immediately brightened and looked like he'd just run into a long lost cousin at a family reunion. I told him that I had recently opened a new small business called Soul Day Spa. Believe it or not, he asked, *"Have you ever been in ESSENCE magazine?"* When I told him no, he suggested that I email a particular person and mention his name in the subject heading. I didn't think twice about it but I thought he was nice enough, and I was happy that I spent a half hour coming out and meeting a friendly face.

About two months later, I was sitting at the front desk at the salon taking appointments and checking people in and out. I distinctly remember the phone started ringing continuously. And that was an anomaly because things had been like the poor flowers in my garden...dead. However, one person after another started calling for an appointment. I had no idea what was going on. Then someone called and said 'I saw you in *ESSENCE* magazine and I wanted to immediately make an appointment.' *ESSENCE* magazine? What was she talking about?

I was sure she was wrong. Then another person called and they said the same thing. In fact, our spot was mentioned as one of the top spas in the country. I was floored! The wave had begun. We got so many calls for appointments, I literally had to install another telephone line in the salon to keep up with all the calls and appointments. In the words of Mr. Powell, the power of PR and relationships is mad real, Yo!

One of the biggest lessons I got out of that was the importance of wonderful relationships, especially with those in the media. I will never forget how my relationship with the DC radio station WPGC began. I had been in business a couple of months and wanted to see what advertising was available on the radio. So I set up an appointment with the sales rep at WPGC in their Lanham, Maryland office. The sales rep was really nice and he showed me all the bells and whistles and then he showed me the rate sheet. And my eyes bubbled like the little emoji cartoon character. I immediately knew that I would not be a client anytime soon because those rates were astronomical. But I was there in the morning and I happened to get there during the time that Donnie Simpson was going off the air for the day.

For those not in the DC area, Donnie Simpson hosted Video Soul, the 1980s show on BET, which was the early peer to MTV. In radio, he is legendary in the DC Metro area. Everybody listens to Donnie Simpson, so his influence is real. The sales guy must've sensed my geekdom a mile away and asked whether I wanted to meet Donnie Simpson. You think?

We walked around to Mr. Simpson and his bright green eyes were glimmering and smiling just as bright as they could be. We went into his office, which was filled with pictures of all kinds of icons. Michael Jackson. Lionel Richie. Stevie Wonder. Every legend you could imagine was on that wall, shaking hands and smiling with the 'green eyed bandit' himself. But what I remember most about those few moments was how gracious and humble Donnie Simpson was. He was genuinely a very nice dude. And he seemed to be very impressed that I had started a small business. I thought that was something considering his wall of fame, but I was just happy for the moment and went on my way.

By the time I was on the road back to Soul, the sales guy called me back. *"I don't know what you said to Donnie, but he said he wants to blow you up on the air tomorrow morning!"* I couldn't believe it. The next morning, I got up at the crack of dawn and turned on my radio. Sure enough, I heard Donnie Simpson say *"you all have got to check out Soul Day Spa and visit my friend, Miss Nicole Cober."* Oh my God, I'm Donnie Simpson's friend?? I thought I had died and gone to heaven!

It was an amazing experience to be called out on the radio, and it really did help me foster a long relationship with the radio station. We did giveaways every holiday. For example, every Mother's Day we would have a *'Queen For The Day'* package and every Valentine's Day we would do a couples package. It was Soul and WPGC. WPGC and Soul. And that was a huge opportunity for a small business to become better known in the community. Between *ESSENCE* and WPGC, Soul was known by the entire DC metro area as an upscale day spa within the African-American community. The power of relationships. The power of the media.

Another lesson I learned about media relationships was the importance of being a part of the community. Rachel's Women Center was a homeless shelter for women in transition within the nation's capital. I met one of the organization's leaders when she came in and purchased a gift certificate for a family member. She was overwhelmed by how beautiful the place was and the good things she had heard about the customer service. We got to talking one day and I mentioned that maybe we could do some services for some of the ladies in the shelter. She thought that was a great idea.

So we set up the day, and I think it was actually one of her press people that wrote a press release about the event. Soon enough, *The Washington Post* was calling me asking to do a story on our *'Queen For The Day'* package. I thought that was a great idea, and I've always been interested in making community service a part of my brand. That was a critical turning point in those early days of building our brand. I was really happy that people thought favorably of us with that story. Mind you, once you get coverage from a large reputable media outlet, then the "pile on" effect begins.

As a result of that *Post* story, we were contacted by *CBS Morning News* shortly thereafter and they also wanted to feature us in one of their "American Hero" segments! Can you believe that? We were American heroes? I was so struck by the irony of that moment. In reality, I was so cash strapped in those days. In fact, I actually watched the story from the inside of a motel room that morning. Why? My electricity had been turned off in my house because I fell behind on payments. The money that I was making was going right back into the business and there was very little left over.

It was so helter skelter that I would either forget to pay my bills or not have enough to pay them. I had another harrowing experience during those early days. I went outside for a lunch break with the intention of driving down the street to pick up some chicken, fries and Mambo sauce (a DC condiments delicacy) from my favorite little Chinese carry out. I went outside but there was no car. The only "carry out" happening that day was by the repo man who had taken my car for missing too many payments! Humiliated. I had to have one of the team members take me to get my car, and my parents came to the financial rescue of their woman/child.

From the beginning, I was sacrificing on my personal essentials for the biz—a story lots of startups understand. So here I was, this "American Hero" with no lights on and no ride, but the world perceived me as not only a hero, but a success. That was always a struggle that I had. On paper and in the paper, I was a success and there was an implied perception of financial wealth and prosperity. However, I was struggling daily to make not only payroll for my team members, but for myself as well.

. . .

In the early days of building the business, I went back to look at my business plan for how I wanted to grow Soul. I remembered how I really wanted to focus on the young professional African-American woman. That was extremely important to me. I built my marketing and sales campaign around that demographic. Howard University was a critical part of my strategic marketing plan. I felt that as a student, the first thing I did when I stepped foot in DC was find the nearest hair salon. And I was broke. Howard University is known for having some of the most beautiful, intelligent and well-groomed women on the planet. My location for Soul was within minutes of Howard University. I put together a few discount cards and placed ads for discounts in the school newspaper. I hired people for the front desk that were students at Howard. My beloved alma mater. Howard. Howard. Howard. And it worked. We had student discount days where students would receive a 20% discount. Soon we had lines and lines of students that were repeat customers.

Speaking of repeat customers, building a clientele is a slow process, at least with the hair salon. Think about it. We are very loyal to our hairstylists and barbers, aren't we? So we had to get deep discounts in those early days of building the stylists book. We also did referral programs where we'd find someone who was really looking beautiful, and if she would refer her friends, she would get a free hair service after her fifth visit. That worked. We also started what was called our standing guests program. Our standing guests would receive a 10% discount if they made a regular appointment for every other week for the entire year. If they made appointments every week, they would get a 20% discount. This was critical to building up our loyalty program. And it worked.

Another marketing strategy that was less successful, at least financially, was Spa Week and/or discounts with Groupon. Groupon and those other discount places were just starting when I opened my salon. They seemed like a great idea at first. The upside was that a lot more people came in. The downside was that the team members hated doing the appointments at a discounted rate. It was a tough balancing act.

Then, there were gift certificates. I remember the first year I thought I had won the lottery from all the gift certificates that we sold. In that first year, I sold about $10,000 worth of gift cards. I thought I was rich. For about three days. I literally went to the Ritz Carlton one night and totally pampered myself for New Year's Eve. I got a massage. I ordered room service (and you know what the markup on that is!) Oh to be young and dumb. So my three days of wealth ended come January 3 when we opened back up. Everybody and their mama wanted to redeem their gift cards, and I didn't realize until then that I had to put the gift card money into a separate account so that I'd have money to pay the team members when they were redeemed. Note to file.

. . .

Social media. I can very simply say there was no social media! I think this is so hilarious to write this; you would think that I opened my business in the age of the dinosaurs, right? But in 2003, Facebook did not exist. Instagram did not exist. Twitter did not exist. But direct marketing did. So I relied on email blasts to tell people A) Who we are B) What we did and C) Why they should come. This worked fairly well. This was how we let our clients know that we were featured in ESSENCE and that we were featured in the Washington Post. It really created a buzz that kept going for a while.

When I said nothing is more important than the time and feelings of our guests, I meant it. I hated waiting in salons. I hated when I came in for an appointment and 12 other people had that same precious appointment. I really, really, really wanted to change that. So I did two things. Number one, we got a computer to make appointments. That way, the front desk totally controlled the books and would not allow double booking to occur. That was awesome.

Also, we wanted to get you in and out. And that meant that we had to have stylists who knew how to work at a steady pace. I did not want people in there for more than two hours for a basic service. And then finally, I needed pleasant people, at least to the customers. I did not want any bad attitudes or trash talking, so I had to set an example. When I found someone getting funky with a client or had a bad attitude or chronically came late, they were out of there. You just had to have some values, right? Mama Barb always says "Say what you mean, and mean what you say." As a business owner, especially when it came to the promises made to your guests, this was the golden rule. Because word travels fast. And bad news travels faster and further.

CHAPTER Sixteen

Mr. Knowles and the Queen Bees (Management and Staff Matters)

Honestly, I believe the heart of my small business were the team members. And I was very comfortable with that. I am not a diva nor did I consider myself a center of attention seeker. I always considered myself to be more like Matthew Knowles than Beyonce Knowles. Like Matthew Knowles before Matthew Knowles and Ms. Tina divorced. The Matthew Knowles that was on his grind to get people to see Destiny's Child, Matthew Knowles. That was me. I was like the agent. And the talent was the talent. The hairstylists and the massage therapists and the nail technicians and the aestheticians were the stars. They were the celebrities. And I was perfectly fine with that. The better they were, the better the Soul brand would be. I knew how to manage the business and the brand.

Therefore, my most important job was hiring good people. I'll say that this was not supposed to be my job. Remember Jana my hair stylist sister friend who was my

Soul inspiration? She was supposed to come in and be my partner. But entrepreneurship is not for everyone. She had a nice clientele where she was and the area in town where Soul was? It too much of a risk for her. I had to be the manager and, as a result, I got baptized by fire.

What was the biggest lesson I learned about hiring? Easy. Don't hire while desperate. You are always going to screw it up. I have hired some zip damn fools over the years, all out of desperation. I remember there was a guy who will remain nameless — let's just call him "Paris." Paris really was an ostentatious dude. The quintessential diva hair stylist with pants on. He had a manager's license, and I did not. Remember I told you how in order to operate and own a salon in Washington DC, you needed a manager's license? Paris had me between a strand of hair and a curling iron.

This fool, first of all, could not hold a curl hostage to save his life. Second of all, he was a chronic and habitual liar. For instance, we were filming an episode of *Ambush Makeover* one day at the salon. Everyone was so excited. But this prima donna was going around to the producers like he was the owner. Telling people to go this way and that... In fact, later I heard that he told people that he was the owner of the salon, and that I worked for him. It got really bad. He was so incompetent that I had to use my favorite words – *"This is not a good fit."* I later heard that he was on some episode of *People's Court*, chile. He and his ex-lover were allegedly fighting over a couch and someone owed someone else some money... It was terrible, and he will forever be known to demonstrate the "Don't Hire While Desperate" rule.

Training. Training your team members is a key and essential management tool. I was very good at a couple of things. Anything that required writing, I had it down cold. Remember my fabulous business plan? Yes, I did that. I also put together fabulous employment manuals. And in the beginning, I really did sit down with people and tell them what our goals were and how to do client intake and all the rest. The challenge, however, especially because I did not have a cosmetology license, was that I really had to rely on my staff's level of expertise in order to be technically proficient. I was very lucky in that regard. One that stands out in my mind — her name was Kathy.

Kathy was a veteran in the DC styling game and she really knew color, and she really knew how to cut and style hair. And so she would train new people that would come on and really help them flourish. Now Kathy did not like a lot of shenanigans, to be sure. She did not like the gossipy day to day crap that went on inside salons. She did not tolerate tardiness. That was a fact. You did not want to get on the wrong side of Miss Kathy with those two infractions. So, after Paris left, Kathy was a godsend and really helped train the hair staff.

My spa staff stabilized as well. I had several team members who were outstanding. Jett was an amazing aesthetician and/nail technician/massage therapist. She could do it all, and some days did do it all. She was a beautiful little lady from Jamaica who had a wonderful daughter and was very reliable. Andrew was another amazing person who also worked there for years. He was from Korea and was an excellent nail technician. However, he wanted to be a massage therapist because they made more money.

Pete was "Mr. Fingers" and was one of the massage therapists. He was every woman's dream massage therapist—long locks, Jamaican accent (not! He was from Southeast DC, I think, but he didn't talk a lot to the clients. He just smiled so they could insert their own "Dexter St. Jacques" voice into their imaginations), very quiet and friendly. Ironically, I never had a massage from Pete. But ladies came from far and near to have a massage with him. He was there for me for years as well. And Kara was another sweetie-peetie who was also a massage therapist with me for a long time. I never had one unkind word said about or come from Ms. Kara. I say all this to say that even though we ran through a lot of team members, we had a lot of stability there as well.

A big reason for the stability within Soul was a lady named Lisa. "Famous Lisa" is what she affectionately called herself. Prior to working at Soul, she worked in the entertainment industry, on Broadway and in Hollywood and styled the hair of famous people--thus the name. Initially, her experience needed a bit of refining. For example, when she came off Broadway to work at Soul, she was used to doing wigs, so she had to learn to lay off the Aqua net. Kathy showed her some tips, and away she went.

She was a five foot nothing, beautiful chocolate skinned lady with a crescent moon sized bright smile. She was legendary in terms of how fast and efficient she was. Her other claim to fame was natural hair. She could get it straight as a bone and still get you out within 45 minutes. She became the standard by which all stylists were trained and measured at Soul. In fact, she was listed by the *Washington City Paper* as *"The Best Stylist"* in DC. I was very proud to have her level of expertise in the salon. She remained manager for more than four or five years I believe.

If there was one thing that was extremely difficult for me: I never like to fire anyone. But I did it for one of two reasons: Either they could not do the work or they did not show up for work. That's it. I know people have elaborate training programs and employment goals etc., and that was true for me as well. But the basic thing that would get you fired is if you could not curl some hair and if you were chronically late to work. I remember the biggest infraction that I had was I hired two front desk people around the same time. Let's call them Tweedle Dee and Tweedle Dumb. Tweedle Dee and Tweedle Dumb were terrible. Why were they terrible? Because they never showed up for work. Within a 45 day period, I think they both showed up to work about 20 days each. The other 25 days, I had to get coverage. It was a disaster. And then they threatened to sue me for wrongful termination. You never showed up for work in the first place, how can I fire you if you never showed up? But I digress.

I also fired people that just were unable to perform services proficiently. Now remember, nothing is more important than the time, appearance, and feelings of our guests, right? So if you could not curl hair within a two-hour period of time, I had to let you go. If you could not get to work on time, I had to let you go. These things were the hallmark of our brand. And the way to enforce your brand is to stand behind your mission statement. Thus, if I had people there who took 12 hours to wax your eyebrows, they were going against the brand. If I had people that roll their eyes at you while you were there, that was going against the brand. If I had people who left you with pimples on your face after a one-hour facial, that goes against the brand.

Those were some of the more difficult decisions that I had to make. They were especially hard for me being a thirty-something who had never managed anyone's schedule before but my toddler's. But you can't build a brand if you don't stand up and hold people accountable. Now, in order to avoid being libelous, I will not name names of all the people who were unceremoniously let go. But we had some funny/horrifying stories. I had two massage therapists, let's call them Frick and Frack. One massage therapist was the elder statesman of the crew. The other one was a newbie—highly intelligent and very enthusiastic. The elder statesman did not appreciate the fact that the young upstart was stealing her shine. To make a long story short, (but not really) they started not speaking to each other. Then, they started speaking in highly irritated voices between massage therapist appointments. One day, I literally saw both of them rolling on the ground pulling massage linens out of each other's hands! On Valentine's Day, no less. Somebody had to go. My 'this isn't a good fit, it's clear you're not happy speech' seemed to work out pretty well in that case.

I also think that you need to have a line of demarcation between being friendly and being friends with team members. It's just a potential disaster in the making. Now, I attended team members' weddings, gave baby showers and acknowledged birthdays and distributed holiday gift cards when financially feasible, but one time, I took it too far. I remember I had a young lady that I really had a lot in common with. We laughed at the same jokes, we read the same books and had the same kind of sensibility. When she was going to California, where I'm from, I even gave her the name and contact information of one my best friends, Nora. Nora was gracious and showed her all around the Bay Area, and the person had a ball. When she came back, we had lots more to talk about.

I sensed that the other team members were in their feelings a bit about our new friendship, but I didn't pay it any mind. When Thanksgiving came around, her family was away, so I invited her over. I vaguely remember her making a comment "So, this is how Nicole lives!" But I didn't give it a second thought. However, the day after Thanksgiving, she had a new attitude. And it was all bad. She started coming to work late and when I asked her to do massages for particular people, she refused. The tension in the room was palpable. One day, she didn't show up on time for a VIP massage, which was highly unlike her. We had to have the 'it seems like you're not happy here, it's not a good fit' conversation. She agreed and she moved on.

Remember the rule I said about not hiring when you're desperate? That clearly applied in my last days of the salon. I hired someone that was a bit...jittery. But she did good hair. No one ever complained. She showed up on time. Until one day, she didn't. My brother got a text from her saying that she was on medical restraint at a hospital for a PCP overdose. I don't know how I never realized that she had a home security device on the ankle! I wished her well, but she understood when I said, (you guessed it) it wasn't a good fit.

There is another story of a young lady who decided to wash her personal laundry on the weekends in our washing machine and dryer. That wasn't enough of an infraction to fire her, but it was a little disturbing. I did ultimately let her go because she was chronically late from moonlighting at her other gig and having clients who she received from Soul come to her and the other spot at a discount.

In the midst of all the firing I did, there were also those who just quit. I remember in the first year of business, I had the three stylists, i.e. "three little birds" quit. Let me give you some context. Because of the lack of startup capital, each week the struggle was real. Remember, I told you I decided to pay my staff salaries rather than on commission. In the beginning, the folks agreed to the salary structure. Until they didn't. Which conveniently coincided with their increased clientele. Let me tell you a thing about math, calculations, and the beauty salon stylists. Now, admittedly, my math skills are basic, rudimentary at best. But when it comes to calculating clients, service totals, commissions and salaries, even Archimedes of Syracuse, one of the best mathematicians of all times, ain't got nothing on a stylist from Washington DC. They know exactly to the quarter how much money is coming in that door and how much they are taking home, and more importantly, how much (or little) my broke ass was taking home. The only part of the equation that they seemed to omit, however, were the expenses.

Now, ladies and gentlemen: What we had here was a failure to communicate. Once we started having a steady flow of clients, the three stylists who helped build that base decided that salary was not the way they wanted to go anymore. BUT, they didn't share that little bit of information with me. Instead, they copied all the customer information out of our computer, found a shop around the corner, and basically moved my hair salon around the corner....without me. If they would have gone old-school, Vaseline on the face, hair back in a ponytail and just beat my ass, it would have hurt less. We worked so hard to just get to that point to make a good name—a strong brand for Soul, and they just bounced. In hindsight, I would like to say that I learned the lesson of hiring often and not taking scenarios like that personally, but I never did. When I counsel businesses now on this principle, I really encourage them to accurately assess the shelf life of the team members and plan accordingly. But small businesses, are notoriously bad at this. We want it to be like a family, all Kumbaya and stuff. Not gonna happen though. Hell, didn't y'all see the *Godfather*??

So yes, there were five or six consistent team members, and there were others that came and went over the years. Sometimes, it just wasn't a good fit. But each person helped build the positive brand while they were there and for that, I'm appreciative.

CHAPTER Seventeen

For The Love Of Money....Financials

Remember I told you about the spa incubator seminar I attended? It was really the foundation where I learned a lot about the financial aspects of running a business. I learned about what a P&L (Profit and Loss Statement) really is. You need to understand what things bring money in for you (i.e. services and products) and what things you spend money on (payroll, rent, utilities and supplies). I also learned about cash flow. Hell, well, I didn't learn about that in class—that was straight on the job training. First, I have no money, yet, I must pay people by next Friday. Where is the cash and when will it flow? That's cash flow 101.

I started learning about the cycles in my business. What days of the week were hot and which days were cold. Marketing was trying to turn the cold days warm or hot. So that's why you see Dominos will run a Monday Night Football special because typically folks aren't buying pepperoni slices on that day. So they create an event to make you buy something on their cold day. Similarly, that's how I started understanding my cash flow. I'd add incentives on Tuesdays and Wednesdays so I didn't just make mullah on Fridays and Saturday mornings. Cash flow 101.

Also, I started prioritizing expenses. Oh yes, there was definitely a hierarchy in who got paid first. By the time I opened, my credit was like Rihanna's song *"Man Down"*...dead, so I did not have a line of credit that would enable me to float the payroll. Terrible financial mistake. I used all my money to just "get open" instead of to operate. This lack of credit would haunt me until the end of days.

Since I did not have credit, I ironically became a great money manager because I didn't have any room for error. My expenses were ordered like this: I can't have a business if I don't pay my team members...they get paid before anyone. Then, I can't have a business if there is no building to work in, so then my mortgage was paid. After that, EVERYTHING was left on the table and paid on an "as really needed" basis, just like in the one-paycheck-away households. We needed relaxer? We would literally have to throw the tub away before we could call Action Beauty Supply. Towels? Put some in the dryer boo because Mr. Spring, the towel delivery guy, was an expense that may not make the cut that month. How about the phone? Well, Verizon was definitely on autopay, but some months were tight. Things like marketing and PR? In the words of the great Tony Soprano, "fuggedaboutit!" I had to do a lot of that on my own, primarily because it fell so far down on the payment priority list.

Another financial quagmire (what a fun word)...Payroll structure. Small business owners have huge issues in certain industries determining whether a hire is an employee or an independent contractor. And the IRS wants to make sure you get it right. Why? I soon found out—the bottom line is who pays the taxes. Period. If you have employees, you pay the taxes. If you have independent contractors, they pay the taxes. Please know that there are bright line differences here, and I didn't know them. Pay attention because this is a huge reason I tanked. I'll tie it all together for you later.

Speaking of taxes, I had an accountant. My accountant did my taxes. My accountant did not advise me on my finances. See what I just did there?? It's called "not slandering" someone. So I will tell you that when it comes to your money and understanding your numbers, ignorance is *not* bliss. So there were lots of interesting things that I could have, in hindsight, required my accountant to do. If I could go back in time, I would have asked the accountant to assist me in identifying cost cutting measures.

If I could turn back the hands of time, I would have said, hey there, my accountant compadre, can you advise me on the financial differences and laws of w2s vs. 1099s? Further, I would have asked him or her to explain what the hell my balance sheet was, why it was important and what I needed it for. A solid accountant should be more than a tax preparer to a small business.

A good accountant should aid the business owner in analyzing the data of the business to help forecast next steps for that business. If I could have given my little self some advice, I would have done these things so much better. See? No litigation will result from this carefully crafted section. (No accountants were harmed in the making of this book!)

Here's the funny thing about getting older. Old adages you totally ignore when you are young and ignorant...they start making A LOT of sense the older your behind gets. Case In Point: There is an old expression that describes my bank loan. Well, two. One is: *"All money ain't good money."* The second is *"If it looks too good to be true, it probably is."* You see? Youth is totally wasted on the young. There! See! A third. Our elders are wise because thousands, no, millions of them got knocked on their asses millions of years ago and then said *"Yo! Don't do that!"* I'm now looking back at my young overly excited behind and shaking my head when I write this part. But here it is.

Remember I told you about the wonderful bank that gave me a loan for my dreams? Remember I was so elated to just have some money to build and to start? Well, there was a *"tickle in the terms"* (I just made that up) of the loan. Without going into the details, the bottom line was...it sucked. On many, many levels it sucked. I'm sure there are far more eloquent, technical or financially-savvy phrases that I can create for you. But the one that does it for me is, was, and will always be *"it sucked."* And it sucked primarily for one reason.

They gave me a construction loan AND they gave me a separate startup capital loan, to use, as the name implies, after I start...up!

But as with all loans, there are fine print terms. And these fine print terms were as follows: you gotta pay on the construction loan BEFORE construction is finished; i.e. before you start up. The consequences? I had the use my "startup capital" to pay back the construction loan before we even opened. While I had $70,000 in startup capital, because construction ran longer than we anticipated, I had to start using the $70,000 to pay the bank back. Not. Cool. But. True. In actuality, I had a few thousand dollars when I actually opened. You see, the "old adages" are making a little more sense now, aren't they?

In all honesty, we had payroll and cash flow problems from the beginning. Sure, the opening of the spa was a tremendous success. I mean, although we did not have Facebook and Twitter, my email game was strong! We had a lovely turn out. All of the team members were there and ready to get to work. We scheduled appointments on site. The downstairs basement was not finished because as I mentioned earlier we had tremendous drainage problems in that area of Washington DC. For a few months, we only were able to use two of the three floors, which was ok, because hell, we were new so we only had one floor of business. As I shared with you before, it takes a while to build a clientele. Which means it takes a while to generate revenue. Which means that from day one, I had challenges meeting my expenses, including payroll.

In hindsight, I probably shared too much of the financials with the team members. Each week, I would have a little 8x11 whiteboard in the staff room titled "Payroll number," and there would be a dollar amount next to it. $4000, $5000, each week. I would tell the teams members: *"OK, team. I have $1500 in the bank right now. We need X to make payroll. Let's get out there and sell, sell, sell!"* I was like a cross between a Wall Street motivational broker and Denzel in the football fable *"Remember The Titans."* The response? Silence. Their faces looked like the little emoticon with the big *"deer-in-headlights"* expression on its face. Good grief. I kept it 100% real. A bit too real, I suppose. But, they did work with a sista for a minute. Why? Because in the beginning, I started them out on salaries, which was cool for them, especially the hairstylists because they were new and had no clients. So we inched along for a while and we barely, but always, made payroll.

When I look back at what went wrong, much of it had to do with the financials.

PART Three
"EM"*BALANCE.
(*i had to keep with the "em" thing...)

CHAPTER Eighteen

Home Girl Imbalance
"Dance Turned Into A Romance..."
—The Jones Girls

Hey now! I think you have a pretty good idea of how a woman like myself could start and operate a business. That was the professional, "how-to-manual" portion of the book. So now, I'd like to give you some behind the scenes perspectives of my home life. And why the HELL would I do that, you rightfully may be asking yourself. Trust, girlfriend, I too have been waffling back and forth on this as well. But, in truth, my personal life very much impacted my business and vice versa. So in order to give you a complete understanding of how the business ended, these sections are very important. And, I honestly think that a lot of folks experience these challenges, but we don't talk about them. We also wonder how a person can "have it all" and what does that "all" look like. For real. Well, let's take a sanitized peek, shall we?

In 2003, Daniel moved back to DC from New York. He was my on-again, off-again ex-boyfriend who moved to NYC to get his MBA from Columbia. Daniel and Nic. Nic and Daniel. You might as well have renamed us "Luke and Laura" or "Bo and Hope" for all the drama that we kicked out. I met Daniel James about four months after I separated from Clarence in 1998. We met at *First Fridays*, a social group of young African-American professionals who would get together monthly as a "networking" event, which was, in reality, a thinly veiled mating ritual. We met on the top floor of an old club called *The Ritz*. Each level played a different kind of music: reggae, hip-hop, house music, etc. I was on the old-school hip-hop floor—the fourth floor. I was the Aisha Curry of my time...very conservative in the way I dressed: I had on a silk navy blue button-down, long-sleeved blouse, black "slacks" (does anybody use that word anymore?) and some Nine West pumps. I was attractive, dare I say, on the edge of elegant, but nowhere near "sexy." I was never that babe. I didn't want guys to look at my ass first. Ever. If they were interested in my face, maybe they were interested in a relationship that was deeper than a booty bump.

Here comes Mr. James. I was instantly interested. He was taller than me, he had a non-threatening, slightly corny (i.e. glasses) but handsome face. In the Black community, we aren't just "Black." No. We use every adjective available to accurately describe skin tone. In Mr. James's case, he would be a caramel-hued, bronze-y colored brother with a curly (read "progressively thinning") hairline. His build was non-descriptive, not athletic or chubby, just enough where he looked attractive in his clothes. Disclaimer Alert: Now, this is my hindsight storytelling "failing" me. I'm sure I thought he was "fine," But I just can't do it! OK. Back to the revisionist history! (I wish I could insert emoticons here.) He asked me to dance, and all I can remember is that we were dancing for a long time. He was corny, but he really enjoyed the music just like I did.

Oh crap! I just had a realization that I met all three of my exes...on the dance floor. Two at *First Fridays* and all of them were obsessed with music like me. Yikes! I think the music was my little soul's release. I was not uptight or shy when I was getting my groove on. I connected pretty deeply with the music and the man and I also thought it was a safe way to express my sexuality. The downside, in hindsight, was I always fell in love on the dance floor of DJs. You know that song by The Jones Girls, called *"Dance Turned Into A Romance"*? Well that is the theme song for my little love life, I suppose.

Crap. Anyway, we danced, he told me what his number was and I looked at him like he was a fool. Um, here's *my* card? YOU call me. Now, I may be corny and romantic, but I was not, not confident. I never believed in the myth of the shortage of good men. And at a minimum, I didn't chase them. I mean really? Anyway, he tried to play hard and not take my card. I said *"nice to meet you, Daniel"* and spun around on my square heeled pumps to leave. He recanted, took my number, and so began the ~~drama~~ story of Nic and Daniel.

So here is where the legal revisionist history continues...Hey, don't be mad at me. When I looked at my role model for writing, the *EAT. PRAY. LOVE.* author, Elizabeth Gilbert, she conveniently glossed over the details of her divorce, too. I'm sure the first draft was a LITTLE different. Then, she had a meeting with her editor and her lawyer and...changes were made. Me? See, I'm a lawyer AND writer, so I just saved myself a ton in legal fees. Anyway, we will still have a good, non-libelous book, minus most of the Real Desperate Housewives of Falls Church component, so stick with me.

We had an eight year break up and make up relationship. That's true. The time we met, Daniel was an actuary. I didn't even know what the hell an actuary was back then. He explained that he worked on figuring out the mathematical probability of people dying (?) and how it related to their life insurance policies...O.K. Not extremely interesting, but he got major cool points for being smart. Also, he didn't talk very much. He was a great listener. That was great because I talked enough for three people, I'm sure. Especially about the stressful relationship of mine that had just ended. He didn't judge me. (Well how would I know, he just listened.) Our offices turned out to be close to each other, so we had lunch frequently. And again, he quietly listened to motor mouth me babble on and on about all my life insecurities and stressors, which included my young son, my job, and my ex. He seemed like a nice ~~therapist~~ guy and friend.

And then, I saw him at Howard's Homecoming. Wow, my life totally changed.

I'll say this: Daniel never met a happy hour that he didn't like. I was surprised in hindsight about how...social he was. He seemed so quiet and reserved. But honey, when he was out with his "fam" from Howard, he was Mr. Personality! Mr. Good Time Charlie! He was every man, woman and woman's best friend's friend. He would definitely get the party rockin'. In the words of MC Hammer, *"Let's Get It Started"* was Daniel's life anthem (he would hate that song selection). From Wednesday to Sunday, he was OUT. I saw him at Howard's Homecoming in his element: laughing, drinking, dancing, and I fell in love.

Again, I am consistent if nothing else. I had on the most boring little clothing ensemble you ever did see: a gray sweater set from *The Limited* and a long gray skirt (who wears this to a club??). I was just dancing my little heart out and then I saw him. He was like a politician—backslapping, buying people drinks, hugging the ladies, dancing and singing—really, all at the same time. He was like Tony Manero cool, except without the dance moves. I was hypnotized. He was so exciting. I was dancing with some lame-o when we locked eyes. Somehow, he made his way over to me and gave me a kiss! In the middle of the outdoor dance floor at Marc Barnes' *Republic Gardens* tent. I was done! I think he walked away too, and the guy I was dancing with looked just as confused as I did.

. . .

So that's how we met, and those two personas Daniel possessed: calm and...charismatic, held me captivated...and confused for years. From the beginning, we liked to take trips together. In fact, he invited me home to Detroit with him for Thanksgiving one month after we officially started dating. Paris was a great trip as well. On Valentine's Day, no less. For me, Paris was my "crack"—you know, the infamous first high. It's the reason people become addicted, obsessed and lose everything. You spend a lifetime of resources, time and emotions futilely trying to recreate one immensely pleasurable experience.

Don't get me wrong: Daniel had great qualities, and I gave him major cool points for being a friend to Jason. Today, I cringe at how soon my needy lil self introduced him to my son, but in this case, it worked out well because he was always kind and supportive of me as a mother. He was ironically very loyal and reliable when it came to doing things with me and Jason. I remember one Easter, early in our relationship, my Aunt and cousin had brunch at like the Hyatt or something, and I was anxious for him to come and meet them. Twenty minutes go by. No Daniel. Thirty minutes go by. Still no Dan. Just as I was about to write him off, he comes in...I'd say slightly hungover tired from the night before. Was I irritated or annoyed? Yes, but I was more relived that he showed up for us. After we left bunch, we took Jason over to Hains Point, a scenic waterfront area by the Potomac River in DC. We laid out a blanket and let Jason run around for a while, then we all laid down for a nap. Lots to love, lots to be concerned about but as a young divorced lady, I focused on the positive.

But that "Good Time Charlie" persona soon became a little larger and all-consuming than I realized. Daniel and some friends wanted to go into the part time party promoting business. They named their little company *"Touch Me, Tease Me Productions..."* after a song by hip hop artists Foxy Brown and Case. That should have been a big ass, "red flag HERE" day for me, right? But nooo, not Nicole. I wanted to turn a playa into a papa or partner. So I focused on his good qualities. But alas, those other issues were consistent; the partying and playing drove me cray-cray.

Also, I'm competitive and ambitious. If I saw him chatting with another lady at the club, I'd start a cuss fest. Or, if he was dancing with another babe, I'd ignore him for a week. Yeah, right, I made bad decisions. Some days I would strongly say *"It's a wrap! I'm not F'in with your ass anymore."* But then, he'd write me a well written, sincere email about how sorry he was. Or, he would ask about Jason or how I was dealing with Clarence, and I'd soften. Or (this tactic always worked), he would invite me and Jason to an activity. A baseball game, for example. Or, he would be by my side at one of the 900,000 child custody hearings I had with Clarence. Just writing this takes me back to those frightening and tumultuous times and Daniel, for better and not so good, was a physically and emotionally supportive force in my life back then.

CHAPTER Nineteen

The Tax Man Cometh

Because the marketing and PR efforts started to kick in, after about nine months or so, we were starting to see repeat business and we were doing a lot better. Not outstanding, considering all the expenses, but better. As you can imagine, if I had $1500 in the bank and the payroll was, say $4000, if we were successful in getting to that $4000, it was a win with a small "w," right, because payroll was clearly not my only expense. I had a mortgage and...I had taxes. As our revenue increased modestly, I could get a bill or two paid. Not all the time, and not at the same time. I had to make some choices. The way I thought about it, payroll was priority. If I didn't have services or service providers, nothing else mattered. I got behind with Uncle Sam. In order to pay down that debt, I had to look at my only asset, my condo. It had a lot of equity. The stress was real. It also coincided with Daniel returning from New York.

Daniel was increasingly stressed about what he affectionately called "the money pit " —i.e. Soul. He was back in DC living in corporate housing for a bit, while the other half of the time he stayed with me and Jason. He also loaned me money from time to time with the business. I think he always thought it was a good concept, but financially adventurous is not a phrase that I would ever use to describe Daniel. He was always the numbers guy. Now, he never looked at my numbers for whatever reason. I really don't know. But he would tell me different things I should be doing, like refinancing the crazy terms I had on the loan, etc.

Around 2005, about two years into the business, I started getting little letters in the mail. From the IRS. *"Dear Ms. Cober, you haven't paid your payroll taxes since you have been in business. What's up with that, dude?"* I'm sure it was something to that effect. I'd trash them, pursuant to my "Ostrich in the Sand" methodology of crisis management. I'm being flippant, yes. Oh it was quite the stressor. I thought, Ok, I will totally pay them back as soon as we have enough cash flow. I literally remember the day that the tax (wo)man cometh. She literally walked in the door one day as I was at the front desk, checking out a guest. Her name was Officer Roberts and she was coming to collect. Well one of the disadvantages of owning a business in the nation's capital is that the IRS's federal and local offices were right down the street. Damn, I thought. Is this what these fools did on their lunch hours, just stroll on in to the small businesses and collect? I literally felt like passing out.

But I agreed to meet her in her office (literally two blocks away...WTF!) to go over all my outstanding liability. Oh yes, it was a hefty little sum. And I had no income or savings...except the equity that was in my home. Gulp! So one of the big retro red flag moments was when I sold my house in order to pay down my taxes. I really was going through all the scenarios in my head. First, I could just sell the house and pay the debt off, but that means I would be homeless. I could work out a payment plan but once they knew I had property, they would put a lien on it. Or, I could talk to Daniel about what our life plans were looking like and see if it included buying a home together. I opted for C.

I sold my condo and paid most of my Uncle Sam debt. Also, I paid for half of the down payment on the new house with Daniel with the balance. Why did I do that? Was it love? Was it a wonderful and financially savvy investment decision? Deep breath honesty moment. It was a two for one...a desperate and manipulative moment. The reality was that I believed that if I didn't pay down my ginormous and exponentially growing tax bill, the business was going to close, and I am way too stubborn to...fail, right? Plus, Daniel and I had been dating on and off for a generation, and we were not any closer to getting married. Frankly, that pissed me off. I mean, I am an amazing woman, right? What is the problemo? What is he waiting for, I thought? The one-sided conversations were endless about whether or not he was moving back and when he moved back, what was going to happen with us, etc.

Now, we hadn't been in the same city for several years and I considered that an investment of my time and energy, and what would people THINK about us NOT at LEAST living together...you see were this is going, my friend? Now sistas, do not leave me hanging on this one. How many of us have spiraled about WHY a brotha won't commit. You know you've done it and so then we start...scheming and thinking and plotting EVEN if the relationship has big ass Dunkin Donut holes in it. So shoot me! Yes, I suggested that we buy a house together and kill two spirits birds with one stone. I can get my beautiful dream house in my beautiful neighborhood with the excellent school district for Jason and...pay down my tax debt. I am the queen of shaping the narrative and persuasive debating. Jiminy Crickets! Do you all deserve all my soulful honesty?? Haha. Yes, you do, so you won't do it too.

So Daniel agreed. I got my house. Uncle Sam went away for a minute. And I got a relationship that went from looong distance, every now and then, to waaay close up.

CHAPTER Twenty

The "Proposal"

Once the tax issue was at least partially resolved, the spa was finally starting to settle down. Things were OK. Not amazing. But ok. We started using the payroll service Paychex in 2006—that was a huge indicator for me. We actually made enough to pay both the team and the taxes—success was defined! Also, around this time, our team members started to stabilize. Our key squad, our starting lineup, was formed. And they were getting good paychecks on a regular basis, so that was good too. Another measure of my trickle down success? We could have a Christmas party—catered by a local small business. An awesome soul food Christmas dinner with greens, mac n cheese and sweet potatoes—yum! The team members and the customers were all invited and it was really a marked sign that things were ok. I still had no credit, however, and we were always one paycheck away from being out of business, but we were hanging in there.

On the home front, once we got into our dream home, I really felt like I had a nice little life. I had a bit of money left over from selling my condo, so I really tried to make our little house a home. I decorated each room — *Crate n' Barrel* here I come! I enjoyed being an *HGTV* wannabe with Jason's room — it was basketball orange and blue jean blue — his two favorite colors. He was settling into Haycock Elementary School for the third grade. The school was a magnet school, had outstanding teachers and was a gold star school in Fairfax County, Virginia. While I was still having issues with his dad about drop offs, pickups and football practices, etc., things had settled down on that front too. I had obtained a phenomenal attorney, Dorian, a Gabrielle Union look-alike, who helped me obtain sole legal custody of Jason. This allowed me to make decisions for Jason about schooling and reduced the back and forth debates that plagued me and his dad for so long. So by all accounts, things were looking ok. Not great, but...ok, no they were pretty awesome, actually.

Except that Daniel still wasn't any closer to asking me to marry him. It made me feel "some kinda way." I'd been with him so long I needed to know where this was going. All those feelings of uncertainty bubbled over on my birthday trip to Cancun in 2006. I just KNEW he was going to propose! Was absolutely sure. I mean, I had "hung in there" all those years of him getting stuff out of his system, I rationalized. We had a nice little life that wasn't bad. I mean why didn't he want to get married? Plus, I mean what about Jason? Shouldn't we all be a family? As we were in Cancun soaking up the sun and sipping the sangrias, I became so distracted by what was not being said (no proposal) that I drank more and more and more.

By the time midnight of July 1st struck, I was in total and complete panic mode. I was crying, sobbing beyond control. I could not understand why there was no ring. So I did what any unhinged 30 something woman does—I gave him an ultimatum. I basically said I need to know where this is going or I'm done. And I think I passed out in a drunken stupor. The next morning, we went down for breakfast and pretended like nothing happened. After breakfast, we walked out to the beach for our little sunbathing ritual. He then proceeded to succumb to my pressure, got down on his knee and asked me to marry him, without a ring.

What a perfect story to share with everyone (this was before Facebook). I remember talking to Cori. Cori was our black 30-something Martha Stewart of the crew. Before the trip, she was like, *"he's going to ask you." "I know it."* So I was elated to share my edited proposal story with her and everyone who asked. Details of drunken stupor ultimatums and ring less fingers were deleted and modified. She and I squeaked and squealed for hours. The issue of children came up and we...I mean I concluded that I should go off birth control IF we wanted to consider having kids. I was 35 already, so we'd have to start soon. Yep...cray cray.

If I wanted it, Daniel was fine with it. He really never challenged me on those types of things. Maybe it was because he was the youngest child in his family and I was the oldest in mine. I was very clear ~~controlling~~ about how things should be. I mean, my parents had been married forever and I had a happy childhood so who didn't want that, right? I was preggers by the end of the month.

CHAPTER Twenty-One

Under Pressure...

"Pressure...pushing down on me
Pressing down on you, no man ask for
Under pressure that burns a building down
Splits a family in two
Puts people on street."
--Queen& David Bowie

et's just talk about the pressures of running a business that is in the red, while being pregnant and understaffed. It was 2006, and I really was trying to have it all. I was making it all happen. I was making a wedding happen. I was pregnant and trying to do that while simultaneously trying to operate a business. Those things are difficult to do in and of themselves. And as I told you, my relationship with Daniel was always strained and moving in together magnified the distance that existed between us. But I used the occasions i.e. planning a wedding, an engagement party and a baby shower, to mask all the challenges that really existed between us. I think this is what you would call a 'dramaholic.' I never stopped to look at whether this was really the right thing to do. I just looked at it from the outside. Well of course we should get married, we've been together (on and off, off, off) for so long. How many of us are guilty of appearance "analysis"?

I never looked at the factors that should exist within a marriage to see if they were present. I didn't look at whether I trusted this person. Whether I worked well with this person. I knew that I loved him. I knew that he was good to my son. I knew that he helped me with my life and that, in a way, was supporting me. And so I thought that that was enough. I overlooked a lot of big things to get my "happily ever after."

And let me tell you a little bit about being a divorced, single person, who's a mom. Well, it always made me feel like I wasn't good enough. A few years earlier, I had a group of girlfriends. And we were all in our 20s and early 30s. We had aged out of the club scene but still wanted to do nice activities together. So slowly but surely, people started getting married and started having children. And let me back up and say these girls were bad. Not bad meaning Bad, but Bad meaning Good, ala LL Cool J. They were all drop-dead gorgeous, all different hues of beauty. Actually, they did have that long haired, light-skinned thing going on now that I think about it. But I didn't hold that against them...(smile). But, I was the only one that was divorced with a kid. I had the same jobs as they did, most were attorneys etc. I had the financial resources that they did.

But not being married really made me feel left out of all of the reindeer games. I wasn't invited to go on trips where the kids *and* the hubbies would be. Just the girls' night out activities, when they were getting away from the husbands and the kids. I don't know if that was an intentional diss. As a matter of fact, I'm sure it wasn't. But I do think that people who have things in common naturally gravitate toward each other. And I just feel like I didn't fit in because I was divorced...with a kid...and attractive.

In my earlier single days, I know it caused me to be in situations I didn't want to be in. Occasionally, before my pregnancy of course, I would see some of the married guys out, sans the wife. And that would give me a little pause. And sometimes, when those husbands were imbibing on some Ketel One vodka here and there, they would make comments about how...fine I looked. Even once or twice, I would see a husband or two with other women who were not said wives, looking a little...cheaty. Disturbing!

In fact, at one political happy hour fundraiser I attended, a guy was so drunk he grabbed me by the waist to say "hi" and sloppily slurred in my ear that he wanted to do a threesome with me and the wife — who happened to be in the daggone room! I broke the hell out of there like the chicken pox. So in my mind, this status...kicked rocks! I wanted to be where the wives and the families were! On the sunny side of the street, I ignorantly thought. I wanted to be a Wife. I didn't want to be privy to no after-hours hubby shenanigans. I felt like I was on the wrong side—the outside. Looking back now, I don't know why I thought that marriages with possibly unfaithful husbands were enviable. I didn't focus on that part. I focused on the not-the-outsider-and-alone part.

Plus, I didn't grow up around a lot of older people who were single with kids. My parents were and still are married, and they had about twelve couples that they hung around with all the time. All us kids grew up together. They would have weekend card parties, birthday parties where the adults would be downstairs, dancing and drinking and partying to Marvin Gaye and The Isley Brothers, while the kids were outside or upstairs playing dolls and tag and things that kids do. That was my utopia. That was what I believed life should look like.

And the fact that I didn't have that life made me feel like I was not enough. I hated that I was not able to give my childhood to my child. Whenever I would see my friends who were married with kids, it did leave a little pang in my heart and a bruise on my ego. No, that's not true. I'm sugarcoating. Girl, it hurt and I was J.E.A.L.O.U.S. Why not me?? Even if those foolios were or may be cheating on their wives...I didn't focus on that part too deep. I was tired of struggling alone and being out on the pathetic, spirit killing dating scene. I was still feeling like my child deserved a nice, illusion of a childhood. I had everything but what I really wanted — my stable childhood...again. And Daniel did love me and

I did love him. We had been together (on and off, off, off), right? So I thought making this work would be good for him, good for me, and good for my son since I hadn't been able to give him that nice home life, in my mind.

When events in our personal life showed signs of melting, I just tried to pack it back together, like when you were a kid trying to make a snowball after the temperature rises—you just keep packing, packing, packing the snowball firmly, trying to force that ever dripping material to stay together. That was me.

. . .

Now, let's also focus on the pregnancy. I obviously hadn't been pregnant in over a decade. So when I got off the pill at Cancun, I didn't think there was a chance in hell that I could ever get pregnant so fast. My planning mind went as follows: We'll get engaged on my birthday and then will have a year engagement and plan to be married next June. Then a year later, I'll make sure our relationship is still OK, and then I will probably have to do in vitro because I'm older but it'll be all good and I'll be ready for a baby. Well, God had other plans. I was pregnant by the end of July. I didn't realize it until about September though. And when I learned the news, the first person I told was Cori. And it turns out that surprise! she was pregnant too. I couldn't believe it! She and her husband had been married for a few years and were trying to get pregnant.

Since I'm such an occasion-planning, excited individual, this kind of living did not seem totally crazy, per se. Cori and I talked every day about weight gain, whether to do an amniocentesis or not, how much we were exercising, names, baby rooms, everything. It was crazy, and I was ecstatic. I got a lot of glee out of trying to figure out how to keep my wedding date on track. And still fit into my previously selected wedding gown. I was getting everything I wanted, all at the same time. I believed I was happy. But, in retrospect, I don't know if I was more happy about being pregnant *with* Cori than I was about actually being married *to* Daniel.

. . .

Now that happiness (with a little delusional "h") describes my personal life. At the salon, it was another story. Around the end of the year, there were several things that turned out to really impact the salon. Number one, the owner of the parking lot next door put a big gate up and sealed off anyone from parking on the lot. I tried to call the owner literally hundreds of times: I begged, I pleaded, and I offered to pay him. Nothing. He had received so many complaints about vagrancy, illegal dumping, cars illegally parked, dead people in the lot, (seriously!) that he thought it was no longer in his best interest to maintain the lot, and he just shut it down. I was devastated.

The area had still not "up or come" anywhere. And the only way that we could get many people to come was that they did not have to walk anywhere in that neighborhood. It felt like overnight the business started tumbling. People would park on the street and if you know anything about the meter maids in DC, they are like gangsters. Mafioso. They would ticket you almost before you even got out of your vehicle. Customers would have boots on their car when they came out of the service. Our team members were forced to ride the bus or metro because they couldn't park their cars the entire day. I begged the city to help me obtain some parking spaces. Nada.

Another thing that the DC government did that nearly killed my business from the beginning was improperly tax the business at a higher rate. Specifically, every year around June, I would get an enormous property tax bill. And if I didn't pay it, I would be shut down. It was so high that it almost took away my profitability margins from day one, if I ever had any. Sometime around this year, I got a bill that was substantially lower than previous years. I called the Office of Tax and Revenue to determine what happened. It seems that they had overcharged me as a non-renovated building for several years. But, they wouldn't give me a credit for what they overcharged me. It was insane. I had one friend in the government, who was a sorority sister of mine, who helped me resolve the issue. Never mind the fact that I knew the mayor and we were classroom buddies. But he did work with me to finally, after months and months and months, get some offset of that. This DC tax issue compounded the problems that I was facing with my cash flow.

I was fighting on another front as well. I had a team member who came from another state as a stylist. He didn't have his DC license initially. I walked him through the steps to get his license, and brought him on.

He's very talented, and I could really see a pickup in business as a result. OK, cool, I thought. I could offset some of the loss that we were experiencing with the lot being closed through the uptick in the clientele that he was retaining. Oh no, no, no, Nicole. You must know that life does not work that easily in a salon. When I was about six months pregnant, he sent me a text message, during one of my prenatal visits, saying that he was quitting and he was taking his clients to start his own salon, again, right down the street from me. Really dude, seriously?

I started having to figure out how to supplement the income that the salon was losing. And plan a wedding. And take care of myself and my little pumpkin. And make sure that Jason was transitioning in school smoothly. And ignoring the fact that Daniel was MIA in planning the wedding.

I was under extreme stress during this time because the ends were not meeting up. Daniel's income was definitely not enough to support our mortgage, our home bills, and the loss the salon was suffering. I knew a few friends that were attorneys who worked on temporary assignments as contract attorneys. I'd never tried that or even knew that was an option. I put in an application, and was rejected. Why? Because I didn't have contract attorney experience. I had been an attorney for four years. I clerked for the DC Court of Appeals for a few years, but apparently I did not know how to work in damned Relativity, a software program for electronic document review, so I was unqualified.

I was humiliated. And stressed. Here I had to plan a wedding that I wasn't really ready for, plan for a child, and find a gap filler to pay employees because of the loss of business we were experiencing. I saw that one of the contract assignments was with my old law firm. In order to get that job, I had to humble myself, call the managing partner in the litigation department, who was always very kind to me, and ask him if I could work as a contract attorney on this project. He remembered me, said of course, and I got the job. I remember being a jumbled ball of emotion. I was happy to have a way to make some good money, but I was so humiliated that I had to go back to the place that tanked me to ask for a position that wasn't even on par with what I used to do, quite frankly. But, in the Tim Gunn, make it work methodology of life that I was living, I did just that.

During the week, I was working a full-time job now and I used that money to make payroll. In the evenings and on the weekends, I was working at Soul. And I did anything and everything I had to do in order to keep the doors open. If I had to do facials, I would waddle into a room and do facials because a team member was on disability. If I had to work the front desk, I worked the front desk. On any given Sunday, I would be carrying 5 gallon Deer Park water bottles up and down two flights of stairs, and sitting at the front desk scheduling appointments, and running over to the bank to deposit cash so that payroll checks would clear, only to then run to the IRS before its office closed to make payments on the back taxes that I owed.

Oh yeah, and after work, work, I'd dash to Virginia, pick up Jason from daycare, do homework and cook a semi nutritious meal, clean him up, throw him in the bed like a football, and then sit on my computer picking out seafoam blue and coral themed invitations for my destination wedding. I felt like I was Ray Liotta's character in the movie, "*Goodfellas*," you know, at the end of the movie, just before he got caught? There was this frenzied montage where the director shoots a series of scenes from his insane daily "to do" list: snortin' cocaine, driving to drop off some guns to Jimmy while watching the FBI helicopter in the rearview mirror, and...making spaghetti for his family?? That's how I was feeling, but I really did not have time to think about how crazy it was.

There were some small signs that my life was coming unhinged. But it would always be someone else's observation. For example, my childhood, forever ever best friend Renee came to visit me. She was an amazing woman, and we had been friends since the ninth grade. She was an engineer and built satellites for a living. Yes, seriously. One day, I picked her up from the airport because she was in town for a couple of days to try on some bridesmaid dresses with me. She noticed that in my car, my Mercedes CLK320, my glove compartment door was broken. How did she know that? Because on this silver grayish interior, I had placed a big fat strip of duct tape on the door in order to keep it closed. That's right, duct tape. It was the same color... I guess that's what I was thinking.

I didn't even think about how insane that must have looked. I didn't have the money to fix it, and I didn't have time or energy to care. She just looked at me and asked me if I was OK, and was I really happy. Of course! Why wouldn't I be? I have it all! Yeah but, your glove compartment...is held up with duct tape. And I think that my beautiful Renee sister did her Renee thing, and went online, found the part, and I had someone put it on for me. She just helped me—didn't judge me or shame me. Just helped me. I cried and chalked it up to being hormonal. I think that stands out to me as a time where some of the little balls began to drop, but I was in my wind tunnel of activity, so I couldn't slow down enough to think about it all.

CHAPTER Twenty-Two

Shenanigans...

At home, there were signs that my relationship was on life support. There are always signs. He started coming home later. Missing a dinner here and there. Usually on a Friday, I could count on the fact he wouldn't be home after work. A happy hour. Rhonda and what's his name's house for a drink. Blah, blah, blah. Then, the Friday happy hours turned into Tuesday, Wednesday, and Thursday happy hours. That's when even Jason, my 9 year old, began to ask questions.

> *"Where is Daniel, momma?"*
> *"I don't know baby. Eat your dinner."*
> *"Is he still at work?"*
> *"Baby, I think so. I'm not sure. Please, finish your chicken."*
> *"It's dark though. He can't still be at work."*
> Silence.

"We only eat chicken because of Daniel, so he should really come home and eat it."
"Jason! I'm not playing with you. Eat!"

I exhaled slowly. Jason, like most kids, is far from a fool. And, he had the uncanny ability to verbalize all the things I was thinking, but not saying. He and I both noticed Daniel's increased absences. I hated that I would get short with him, when Daniel's increasing absence was the real target of my frustration.

One of the most painful moments happened shortly before the wedding.

"Hey, Daniel. It's me. My office is closed for the holiday, so I was thinking maybe you could come over and kick it with me. Call me back."

That was the message some person left my "beloved." I honestly don't know why I checked his message that time. Well, that's not entirely true. I hadn't fully trusted Daniel from about three months into our on-again, off-again eight year relationship. Once trust issues infect a relationship, it's like gangrene. Sooner or later, you got to cut the limb off. But my tenacity has always been both the blessing and curse of my personality. I hate to quit. I don't like to fail. I am going to make it work. No matter what.

I was driving home when I called Daniel. It was Friday evening, so I was pretty sure of two things: one, he wouldn't answer the phone and two, I'd be waddling home to an empty house. That's ok, though, because I had so much to do for the wedding. Jason was normally with his father in Bowie on the weekends. That meant that I'd be by myself because undoubtedly in DC there is always some happy hour, reception, mixer, another frat-brother-in-town-on-Fridays gathering for Daniel to attend.

As I worked my way through the evening traffic, his voicemail came on: *"You've reached Daniel at 123.456.7890. Please leave a message, and I'll get back to you."* Beep. I had three choices: 1. leave a message; 2. hang up or 3. hack into his phone messages.

I had to make a decision quickly. Was I prepared to deal with the fall out if I heard something bad? But things were going well. Were things REALLY going well or were you turning your head the other way? I engaged in a quick yet substantive debate with myself. But Nic, here you are, in Falls Church, Virginia, in a beautiful two story, 3,200 square foot home, driving your CLK-320 Mercedes Benz, and most importantly, Jason is happy and in a great school system! You have a successful business too! You are getting married and will have the stable family life you deserve. That's what you grew up with. That's what Jason deserves. That made perfect sense. Why go looking for drama? Just keep it movin'...Impulsively, I put hacked the damn phone anyway.

When I heard the message the first time, I felt my belly tense up really, really tightly. Then I felt a throbbing sensation radiating around my right shoulder and all around the back of my neck. I listened again, as if to say, maybe you heard it wrong. Why oh, why do folks overanalyze the obvious?!

"*Kick it.*" First, you dismiss the smallest irrelevant detail. "What grown ass woman says, "*kick it?*" Then after the 5th replay, I felt drunk. Lightheaded. Dizzy. Then there was a "*thud*"! I hit the Mazda that was in front of me. It was bumper to bumper traffic, however, so what I thought was a thud was actually not worth getting out of the car. It was just enough to jolt me out of the haze I was in. The driver gave me the finger, I apologized, and refocused. "*Just Lord please get me home, get me home, get me home.*" Focus. I muttered to myself. I didn't cry. I didn't yell. One hand on the wheel, the other on my belly. I just rubbed my belly over again, and again and again. "*Happy, healthy, smart.*" "*Happy, healthy, smart*" would be my mantra all the way home. When I was pregnant with my oldest son, those were the three things I prayed for.

But what my soul ached for was to give my child and my soon-to-be-born son the loving, supportive, stable family life that I grew up with. I had sooo much guilt and shame that I was already divorced. I had failed miserably the first time. The thought of another failure almost stopped my breath. Instead, I started to breathe so deeply and so strongly and quietly and I repeated my prayer over and over and over again until I arrived safely to the complete emptiness of my house. I parked my car, turned off the car lights and sat. It was about 36 degrees outside and the D'Angelo/Lauryn Hill song, "*Nothing Even Matters*," played softly in the background.

In spite of the nearly freezing temperature, my cheeks were flushed. I didn't blink for the entire song it seemed. Even as the drops of fear and disappointment rolled down my face.

In my earlier days of our eight-year disunion, I would just blow the hell up at him. Yell! Cuss! Break up! And the worst war—silence! Before we lived together, any of those acts would illicit professions of undying love... *"Please, baby, baby Please. You are wrong. You're not being fair! You only look at the bad things. You are so critical. You don't appreciate the things I do for you. For Jason. I love you. I love Jason. I want us to be a family."* That would always make me pause. Stop. Reflect. Maybe I was wrong. I really wanted that above all else. A family. Stability. An environment that was good for my son. Once we moved in together, however, things dramatically changed. He made less and less effort to connect with me.

Maybe it was my fault for checking his voicemail. Things had been going relatively well. I guess. After a courtship of eight very long soap opera-like years, Daniel and I were finally getting married. *Finally.* So I wiped my tears and kept quiet about the message. I went in the house and turned on the computer. Numbly, I scrolled on www.theknot.com for welcome gift options for my wedding guests.

CHAPTER Twenty-Three

Coley Bear

Cole was born on April 10, 2007. This was a month or so after the shenanigans with Daniel. And two months from our wedding date. With Jason, I had a C-section and I was determined that I wanted a vaginal birth this time. Determined, primarily because I could not see how in the hell I could be away from the salon for any real period of time. That morning, I was starting to get some mild contractions, but nothing was happening. My doctor was not an advocate for a vaginal birth after a C-section, which totally pissed me off. You see, I have a conspiracy theory about C-sections. It's not rational, and may not be based in any scientific literature. But I think that these daggone obstetricians want to get off to their tee time and want to schedule as many births as possible for liability reasons and convenience. It really pisses me off! So, I was trying to be controlling and do the vaginal thing. But at a certain point, my doctor said that I could risk rupturing my old sutures from my previous C-section. Great, I thought, yet another monkey wrench in my plans.

I had a C-section, but I thought, since I was totally Miss Bikram yoga and all that, I could pop right back into shape. This would be different than ten years ago, I thought. Nope, nope, nope. I remember it like it was yesterday. The doctor said that I would need at least six weeks of recovery. My mom and Daniel were there in the room when the doctor told me, and I literally started bawling like a baby. Well, actually not like my real baby, Cole. Because he didn't cry. I was just crying like a fool by my damn self. Not because I was happy about my baby. Not because I was in any pain. It was because I was stressed up to my eyeballs about how could I make this whole thing work at the salon and not be there.

What added to my stress was the fact that the doctor didn't close me up all the way, apparently. You read that right. Let me give you an example. You know how when you're sewing and then you finish an area and you create a knot to seal up the little stitch that you've made and then you snip off the rest of the string? Well my dumb dumb doctor, who will remain nameless for litigation purposes, snipped the knot. So yeah, kinda gross, but my stitches started unraveling. Yep, I still have a little indentation above my "va-jay-jay" region to this day. Here I was, in the hospital for an extended stay, nursing my baby with cracked and bleeding areolas, because you know, that's how nursing begins; sporting one eyebrow because my other eyebrow hairs were shedding after child birth *and* trying to heal an improperly unsealed childbirth wound around my lady parts. With no sleep and little food. Oh, yes-I was a physical and mental mess.

And those, unfortunately, weren't the only difficulties I had to handle. I still had a mercurial business to run. Once I was discharged, I'd sit at the computer, nursing Cole on one boob, on the telephone trying to order supplies, pay bills, and keep the staff from going buck the hell wild. People are great, but absent leadership, especially in a small business, can be its death nail. And no one had sympathy or compassion for my postpartum situation.

As soon as I could walk up and down a flight of stairs, I was back in there. You know, for those of you who have never had a C-section, you have a challenge walking and re-utilizing your muscles that have been cut. Things that require you to use your stomach or your ab muscles are going to be a problem. Like stairs. And I had two flights of them. But, in true Nic form, I put on my black yoga pants and Soul Day Spa T-shirt, and waddled all up in there with my quiet baby at the front desk with me within ten days. I had it all, didn't I??

CHAPTER Twenty-Four

Playa Del Carmen

In June 2007, I put my kids, my family and friends (and the groom) on a plane to Playa Del Carmen, Mexico. Three things stood out to me about the wedding. Number one: My six-week-old baby never cried—he was peacefully observing all the festivities and new faces the entire time. Number two: I felt like Julie the cruise director from the Love Boat at my own wedding, making sure everybody had fun. I was exhausted and everything was a blur. Number three: I did fit into that daggone dress! And by all accounts, I was the prettiest bride I have ever seen. Seriously. No hyperbole. That dress was amazing. It was an *Amsale* strapless column dress and it had feathers on the bottom! I'm telling you, girlfriend, I was a bad bitch. And I couldn't get over all the compliments on how my skinny ass fit into that dress after six weeks. Yes dammit, I soaked up all those compliments, because I wasn't getting any from my husband. It was like we were at two different functions — he was entertaining his friends, and I was entertaining my family. And his. He did not comment at all on what I looked like or whether he liked the event. He thanked his family and friends for coming.

The resort was breathtaking. We stayed at the *Playacar Palace*. It was an all-inclusive hotel, and not one of those raggedy, janky hotels either. The food was outstanding morning, noon and night. We had about eighty guests come from all across the country. They all had an up close and personal view of our eight year soap opera, and wanted to come and witness the big day.

For Daniel's part, I always felt that his family and friends either liked me or pitied me, and thought I was *"good for him."* And that was OK, I supposed. My family did like Daniel. There was nothing not to like; he was a friendly enough guy, and plus, I didn't really share all the back door drama. My mom was so happy that Jason had a stable home. And a stable school life. And I agreed. I just had to keep going. And the wedding was the first step of that keep going. He was a great dad to Cole and Jason. Whereas some men didn't take on that responsibility too well, he did show up for the kids. Maybe not for me, but he did show up for the kids. And I was clear that I loved my kids more than...the other stuff. We didn't actively argue, we kind of co-existed. Or maybe I just gave up the notion that any long term relationship could look any better.

At the wedding, the only time we spent one-on-one was a nice morning where we took Cole out to the beach. That was a happy memory. I could tell he was proud of the way the wedding came together and how well his family and friends were treated. Well, maybe a friendship was good enough...

CHAPTER Twenty-Five

Keep Goin' Gurl

By the time we came back to DC from Mexico, I was now working as a contract attorney not only to pay for my "dream wedding," but I was now putting all of my work money toward the salon. Which in turn meant that all of Daniel's money was paying for us. And, that was a big problem.

Daniel now worked for the CFO's office in DC and financial security was his middle name. Entrepreneurship, however, was not his thing. Let me rephrase: Financially unsuccessful businesses were not his thing. He was a great arm-chair quarterback, though. He was constantly and heavily criticizing me on what he characterized as my financial irresponsibility. For example, one evening, when he found out I paid a telephone bill late, he quite dramatically (and ironically), ripped up the *"5 Love Languages"* book I bought us to work on our relationship. That same night, he proceeded to pull all my clothes out of the closet on the floor...while his mother was visiting us. (She quietly hung everything back up, though.) So yeah, there's that. Yet, when I conceded and pleaded with him to do the financial management of the business, he was nowhere to be found. It was a hot mess.

. . .

Soul's sales took a dramatic downturn. Toward the end of 2007, the economy decided to play "hide and go seek" — it just vanished. With my clients' jobs and paychecks. It was in the shitter. And it hit the salon quite dramatically. Our clients, who were very loyal and coming every week or every two weeks, just disappeared. The spa business was literally cut by 50%. Luxury items were the first to go. Now, I was not only working for myself, I was working literally to keep the lights on and keep people paid. The stress was real. I remember one time (or two) a payroll check bounced. And one of the stylists let me have it. *"YOU are the one that wanted to be an owner, not me. So that's not my problem."* Ouch. I felt as small as the penny that was left in my bank account. Things were getting hot around the salon...and around the globe.

Incidentally, this was around the time that a young, gifted and Black senator from the south side of Chicago started to consider running for President of the United States.

CHAPTER Twenty-Six

Mr. Cober Comes To Washington

Sometime in 2007, my brother Brian, or "Uncle B" as he came to be known, came to DC from California. He had just finished culinary arts school and was a chef at one of the Bay Area's most prestigious restaurants. He had a lot of drama with his ex, however, and wanted to come to DC to try to get a new start.

My relationship with Brian was always more of a maternal one than one of friendship or even siblings. You know the kind: *"Did you do this?" "Did you do that?" "I can't believe you did this!" and "I can't believe you didn't do that!"* He would respect and summarily reject whatever advice I gave. And tell me why I was wrong. We were like olive oil and a lovely balsamic vinaigrette. That's right—we would argue intensely about everything. Relationships. Politics. Life. He was really the only one I had that dynamic with. I never argued with my parents. Or good girlfriends. Or colleagues. Just Brian, and the occasional ex. Even Daniel and I didn't argue. Oh trust me. I would yell, and he'd let me get it out and then he'd tell me why I was wrong and I'd be like "whatever" and move on. Brian, however, was intense and I was intense. And we would cuss and cuss but then one of us would apologize or forget it happened the next day.

Now, let Brian tell the story, growing up, he loved his big sister. We had some funny times! When we were like 6 and 3, I used to suck my finger (not thumb because I was unique) for a very long time. Instead of a using a blanket ala Linus from The Peanuts gang, I would use Brian's peach fuzz, chubby cheeks! I'd make him come stand next to me and I would rub the little peach fuzz! Oh my gosh, he hated it but he loved his sister, so he just stood there with his arms folded and irritated while I was soothed. It's hard to envision it today, but this ginormous, tatted-out "thug life-in-remission" brotha was my human comforter for a moment in our childhood! Honest!

While he may not have loved being my human blanket for a time, he loved the way I always stuck up for him growing up, which I did regularly. My maternal instincts kicked into overdrive with my family: It's one of those things where I can talk shit about him, but cain't nobody else do it. Growing up with Brian was kinda fun. I was like a little mom. Once we were in grade school, our morning ritual was that I would get up and make our breakfast and lunch while mom and dad got ready for work. Then, I'd also "pick" out his little hair. I'd spray it first with a little Afro-Sheen, pick it out (which he hated) and then gently throw a silk scarf over the entire head. Then, I'd pat, pat, pat the silk scarf (with the afro underneath) and slooowly remove the scarf and poof, like a magic trick; he had the cutest little Afro on the block! Well, truth be told, he had the only little Afro on the block as we are the only Black people on the block. However, it was still objectively quite sharp. But I digress.

The archetypes we played in our family were cemented as children. I was the good girl. He was the bad boy. For his part, Brian always added a little entertainment (read stress) to the household. For example, when he was 10, I think, he and his friend sat in my mom's car in the garage and decided to try to drive it. Instead of putting the car in reverse, it went forward (because, of course, he's TEN) and he ran my mom's car into the garage/house wall trying to take it for a joyride with his friend. That didn't end so well.

Brian's charisma and personality embodied the spirit of Oakland. He had a bravado and ego that cared less than four f$%^s. He was never insecure; nor did he try to be anything other than who he was. He kept it ...100, as he would say. And no matter what he did, no one could ever stay upset with him because he was a charmer, a fast talker. I never felt as comfortable in my skin as he obviously was in his tattooed and pierced casing. I admired that deep, deep down, but it was always a stressful quality for my family to deal with.

In his senior year of high school, he ran track for the first time. He was so good that he got an athletic scholarship to UC Riverside I believe. However, that didn't work out too well. Then he went to Morehouse in Atlanta. And partied a little too hard I guess. Which is how he found himself in the military. He went to the Navy and did really well with structure and organization. He found a boo, got married when he got out of the military, but when that tanked, he wanted a new start in DC.

Brian stayed with me one time briefly while he was in the military, and that was a disaster. He was young, wild and free in the Navy and would come and kick it at his "big sister's crib" and borrow her Benz for a fun nightlife on the weekends.

In fact, that foolio is the one who talked me into that daggone car in the first place. "*Nic! You are a baller now, you need a ride that is ballin too! You's a big time lawyer, you know what I'm sayin'? You can't be ballin in no Corolla, dawg!*" Wait what? What's wrong with my little Corolla anyway, I thought, as he drove me and my Corolla to the Mercedes dealership with Jason. We made the horrific mistake of test driving a drop top black CLK320...on 395, a highway in Virginia on the brightest, most pleasant looking day in June. The car gods were conspiring against me from the beginning. Jason, aged 4, threw his hands in the air (and waved them like he just did not care) for the entire ride.

Brian turned up WPGC where Missy Elliott was singing about "getting her freak on" as loudly as the Boze speakers would let her scream. I was driving— shaking my head "no, no, no" but my face betrayed me with a huge cheesy grin. This. Was. Livin! He was right, I stupidly thought. I should treat myself and "*ball outta control.*" So I compromised. For my 30th birthday, I did get the CLK320 BUT without the drop toppedness.

The highlight (or lowlight) of our previous experience was that he wrecked that CLK within a year of me having it. It wasn't his fault (I'm sure...) So when Mr. Cober said he was coming to Washington DC, again, I was a little concerned.

I told Daniel that Brian was coming and true to form, he didn't say much. He and Brian got along well during our break up, make up years. They were two sides of the same coin. Both liked to party. Both liked to "kick it." And were charming with the ladies. I honestly didn't think that it would be a bad thing for him to come and stay with us. Initially, things went very well. Brian was very helpful with cooking for me and the kids. He also helped at the salon periodically. But living with us, he also got to see the inside of my relationship with Daniel. By that time, Daniel and I were more like business partners, or divorced people living together. We had a schedule with who would pick up the kids and drop them off at daycare. We would go to work. We would rarely have dinner together.

In my mind, I rationalized that's probably how most couples were anyway, so I convinced myself that I didn't mind. I just focused on the fact that he was there for the kids.

Brian, however, was like: "*What in THE hell is going on? You guys don't even talk to each other.*" At that point, I was numb. I was so exhausted with working at the salon and going back-and-forth with the kids that I didn't even notice we didn't have a relationship anymore. Quite frankly, I think the proverbial shit hit the proverbial fan when Brian went out one night and saw Daniel. Whatever Brian saw, Brian did not like.

Immediately, he was in my ear about that and it wore me down even more. But, all I cared about was my kids. All I cared about was that we had a nice home. Nice school system. And we both took care of the kids. That was the only way I was really able to keep my sanity. So Brian kept his mouth on mute for a minute. He kept his mouth closed when Daniel would come home late or not at all. He kept his mouth closed and would shake his head if he would see Daniel out without me. Me? I just stayed focused on the kids. And the salon. And the finances. And the taxes. And making payroll. Tensions in the house were brewing like a percolating little teakettle.

Brian was trying unsuccessfully to wake the comatose giant in me. But I was his big sister, so he deferred to my wishes. Plus, I think he knew that I needed that "peach fuzzed, chubby cheek" security again on some level—so he just quietly folded his arms, and stood there, in silent protest--like he did when we were little.

Neither of us realized it, but some reinforcement troops were quickly approaching.

CHAPTER Twenty-Seven

Michelle and Barack...NOT

The ushering in of a new Black president was totally revolutionary. And I'm sure there were more than a few Black households that experienced some unique new tensions on this subject. Why? Because, let's just be very clear: Barack Hussein Obama is the perfect human being, in my humble opinion.

There was one thing that stood out about the President. It was more important than his intellect. It was even more important than his series of (future) accomplishments of bringing the country out of the economic commode, killing Osama Bin Laden, singing negro spirituals, visiting brothas in prison and addressing gay marriage, and immigration and climate change...and Obamacare. To me, Mr. Obama's single most revolutionary act was the way this man loved his wife. This one act created an image of what a loving and successful relationship could look like. And it didn't involve the playa, playa antics that were so rampant in the community (and my house).

But you can't leave Michelle out of the equation. This sista left a clear impression on me that she was NOT having any shenanigans. Not one bit of it. I imagine that if you were to even dream about committing some shinaniganry on Ms. Michelle, from the South Side of Chicago, an assassination attempt would come from within her personally. No Department of Defense assistance would be needed.

So what's my point? My point is that Michelle and Barack RAISED the bar on relationships. Respect. Kindness. Trust. Um, it looked to the outsider that those two embodied those values. Meanwhile, out here in these streets (ok, I'm not out in anyone's "streets" but give me some literary liberties, will you, please and thank you), the brothas got women believing that we should be "a ride or die chick." And trust and believe, in my current relationship, I found myself on many occasions riding shotgun.

While I wasn't quite at the point where I could look at my relationship with a sober eye, I honestly started using Michelle and Barack as my relationship role models, and it was good to see. Yes, I had my parents and that was cool and all. But...I just fell in love with the idea that Michelle and Barack's love was something to aspire to. It made me think seriously about my values and what I was compromising on and for.

· · ·

Daniel and I received tickets to one of the Inaugural Balls. He was in his tux, and I was in a gorgeous black and gold, ethnic print strapless *Nicole Miller* ball gown, with my black and gold *Gucci* shoes (which were literally a size too small, but they were *Gucci*, didn't you hear me?) Our family and friends came from all parts of the country to witness the Obama Inauguration: Mom and Dad from Cali, Cori and Jerry and their baby Ashton, and Daniel's uncles from Florida. For one pure instant, it seemed that we would get our Michelle and Barry moment after all! We walked out of the house like celebrities, with drinks in hand and everybody waving, taking pictures and wishing us well.

However, in the wee hours of the morning, I arrived back home...barefoot with shoes in hand, dress disheveled, mascara streaming down my teary face, without Daniel. On the dawn of the first African American president's first day in office, it was clear to me and everyone around us that our dream had taken a turn down a foggy, dark road that more resembled Kruger's Elm Street than Pennsylvania Avenue.

CEO OF MY SOUL

CHAPTER Twenty-Eight

The Town Center

When I heard about the Maryland Town Center having an available retail space, I got my second wind. The Town Center was located in an affluent Black suburb of Washington, DC. This was my dream location! I really believed that if we put Soul here instead of the dodgy area in transition we were in, it would be the key and ideal location for a luxurious spa. It was housed in the same outdoor mall that had Macy's and Bed Bath and Beyond and Footlocker etc. I could really be in there with the big leagues, I thought. This could be my first step toward my ultimate goal of franchising Soul. If I were successful with having two functional locations, I could start the franchising process. To date, there was still no African-American owned day spa and salon chain. My ambition kicked into overdrive.

The location was perfect. It was right next to Old Navy and, in fact, the previous business in that space was a spa. I started inquiring. In my mind, I thought "more" would be better. If I had more revenue I could make the DC location work and this busy town center would totally give me all the customers I needed that I couldn't get...in the hood. The managing office was even going to throw in incentive money for me to build the space out. How could this not be a sign from God that Soul was going to finally be a chain?? I was convinced that this was my lifeline. This was my opportunity to expand and turn the business around.

Well clearly I didn't read my own novel. I didn't look at the fact that the last rites were being read to my pitiful little marriage. I didn't look at the fact that The Town Center was nearly 50 minutes from my home in Virginia. I did not look at the fact that I had little to no money to operate the new business besides the check that the property management would give me which was supposed to go exclusively to the build out. I also didn't realize that hello! I was not a commercial real estate broker. All of those things are kinda important factors that need to be in place before you decide to expand.

But as is the case with Nicole, I thrived on a ~~distraction~~ challenge. I didn't look at the things that couldn't work, I looked at all the things that could work. I asked Daniel his opinion. He didn't say yes, but he didn't say no either. So we applied and were approved. He opened a Discover card to assist with operating costs.

I had two months to renovate and by now, this process was second nature to me. It wasn't nearly as difficult as 25 Florida Ave was. All I had to do was put down some flooring and some paint, buy some beautiful artwork and furnishings, and find people that could work there. We could be up and going. My oversimplification of success is astounding to me, even to this day...

So now I had two kids that I was responsible for getting around the beltway for. I would drop Coley bear off in Springfield, Virginia at daycare to Marta who was my beloved daycare provider for many years. I would always be so panicked and rushed with 1,345 things on my to-do list that I always remember looking back to see if I had really, in fact, just dropped him off. I see how that happens sometimes with parents. It is horrific to be so stressed with life that you cannot remember whether or not you dropped your child off or not, only three minutes before. I would keep looking in the backseat- one time...two times...just to make sure. Obvious red flags in retrospect.

Then, I'd roll around the beltway to the new location to help with construction management issues like picking out the floor samples and furniture etc. so that we could get open as soon as possible. Daniel would pick up the kids occasionally in the evening, so I could work around the clock sometimes until 11 o'clock at night to make sure that everything was OK.

I put ads online for our team members, and started interviewing and training. I got some really great people to come and work there. By the time we held our grand opening, the place was breathtakingly beautiful.

What was not so beautiful, however, were the terms of my lease. And I hate this, because I'm an attorney and should have known better. Start your finger wagging, tongue lashing, shaming session now. I tried to negotiate my own lease terms. And got hit in the esophagus when the reality hit me. Instead of having a monthly all in rent of $5000 (that means all the utilities and maintenance fees would be included in the rent), my rent was $10,000 a month, all in. These fools were charging me for everything but promoting Jesus's coming back to Earth concert tour.

My utilities were 1000% higher than they were in DC. No hyperbole. I couldn't afford counsel, but I didn't research enough to realize what all of the terms were. All that being said, we STILL opened and made not only rent but our payroll. It was a huge success. That location was prime in the beginning summer months for us.

And my theory worked, initially. The Maryland location was able to make enough money to make the ends meet for DC. Not enough for me to live off of independently, but enough to pay its own expenses. And that was good enough for me.

I also had the benefit of having Brian help out at the salon in DC. And on its face, that was helpful. He allowed me to be in two places at one time. But the staff complained that he made mistakes with scheduling etc. Looking back on it though, I don't think that that was really what they complained about. I think it was just the fact that I was not there, and had a new Maryland child that I was tending to. Also, I know that he was the marketing person that I could never be naturally. Remember how I said that when we were growing up he was Mr. Friendly Fred? Well, that turned out to be very helpful in terms of bringing in and retaining new young lady clients. This man was full on single and ready to mingle. He was like a kid in a Willy Wonka's chocolate factory. He told me later about all of the women he had rendezvous with... I was horrified. Some of the clients? Nice upstanding lawyer ladies...who were married? I didn't believe it. Yep, he said them too. And a team member? Good grief, this was horrible. But I didn't know it at the time, so it didn't kill me then.

The bottom line is that my business dream of becoming a chain was finally a reality. In my personal life, however, I was facing the fact that I was living a nightmare.

CHAPTER Twenty-Nine

"Let's Just Kiss And Say Goodbye..."
— The Manhattans

Having the two salons was absolutely the last thing an otherwise fragile relationship needed. The financial pressures were causing us to cuss and fuss with three times as much frequency and velocity. We had an incident — a really, really bad argument. And for the first time in my relationship, I was scared. Not only of him, but of us. I was scared that our relationship had hit the point of no return. And for all of the sacrificing I did to give Jason and now Cole a nice "normal" life, our relationship was spiraling to the point where if the boys were around that, my biggest fear would be realized-- they would see a desperately dysfunctional couple. I didn't grow up like that, and I didn't want that for my children. I honestly thought we could make it work just by coexisting. I really did. He was doing his thing, I didn't care. As long as we could co-parent together in the same house. I really believed that. But as our arguments started escalating, I panicked that if one or both of the children were to ever see that, they would never be the same. And I knew well enough to know that things were not going to get better.

But I was afraid to leave. My credit score was on death's door. And when we had briefly separated previously, I knew that I couldn't rely on him to cosign on a rent agreement...to leave him. That was crazy. I was so stressed that I didn't even want to apply for an apartment. I didn't have any money. I couldn't ask my parents. And one real thing that kept me there was the salons. I knew that by walking out, not only would my marriage come crumbling down but it would only be a matter of time before the salons would suffer too. I didn't know what to do.

I had a friend at the time who was knowledgeable about the apartment rental market and suggested a place in Falls Church about five minutes from the house. On a whim one day, I completed an application and submitted it. I just knew I wasn't going to get it because of my horrible credit history.

We had a customer appreciation event at Soul and the next morning, I drove all the way out to Landover, Maryland to return some party good rentals we used for the reception. I had put my application in a few days earlier, but I hadn't heard back yet. I was never a big drinker, but on this day, my stress was at an all-time high and was getting to me. I went to the Giant grocery store and in addition to one of those slices of marble cake from the bakery, I picked up one of those little boxes of wine. You know, the single packs that you're supposed to use when you go to happy music festivals during the summer or for a nice picnic or something? Yeah, one of them.

Well on this day, I went in and got it at 10AM in the morning. It was like a little juice box for adults in crisis at that point. I left and drove to the party rental place, and just sat in the parking lot thinking about what I was going to do with my little life. Was I going to stay and watch my marriage devolve into a place that I had never envisioned for myself? Or was I going to have a little faith?

I wasn't a big Bible reader but, I love a short message or catchphrase. Wasn't there something in there about a mustard seed? Like having faith as tiny as a mustard seed? You are pitiful, girl, I thought. Drinking wine, out of a box, before noon? This is not cool. There were so many things wrong with this picture, girlfriend. Just relax. How can I relax!? Everyone around me was telling me to relax. My mom. My brother. I was having a pretty hard time of it, actually. Well, try the faith thing then, I mused. I exhaled, put my wine juice box under my seat, unopened, walked in and returned the tables and chairs that I had rented. When I came back to the car, I had a message on my cell phone. I had been approved for the apartment.

And so on that day, I borrowed money from a law school friend and I used it to put a deposit down on my new apartment. By the next 48 hours, my children and I had moved five minutes away to an apartment of my own. I was ready to have some faith, do my best on my own with no security net of a marriage or relationship. I would see what God had planned and see what I could do to try to keep the salons open as well as make a living for myself and my children. I decided, for better or worse, that peace in my home outweighed my illusion of having it all. In the back of my mind, I was not quite ready to concede that I had failed.

At that point, I even thought I could have sacrificed my own happiness a bit more with regard to my relationship with Daniel. If it were just about our lack of intimacy, I would probably have still stayed, honestly. What I could not risk was our children witnessing our now toxic and vitriolic behavior.

I don't have no tolerance for that. Didn't then; don't now. I didn't move for myself, I moved out of fear for what my children might be exposed to. I didn't grow up around volatile parents. I didn't even know what that felt like. As much as I wanted a family, I didn't want a family under any circumstances.

As the moving truck started on down the street, I followed behind it and saw my home, my dream home, in the rearview mirror like a cliché. I only looked back once. Well, maybe twice.

CHAPTER Thirty

DE(ath) La SOUL

Now I was on my own—divorce papers were filed. I was thankful for my brother because he really was my external hard drive at this time. He and my good friend Noelle came and helped me sweep up all of the stuff that I was taking into my apartment and encouraged me to move forward and not look back. Brian also helped me be at two places at one time. He had a little life change of his own around that time. He found out he was going to be a dad. So he had incentive to really want to make a go of these businesses as well. And again I say we were hustling and making it work. That is until December 2008 and January 2009.

Snowmageddon. The Town Center is a town center, and a town center is outside, right? We had the biggest snowstorm in recent history during that time. It forced us to close for days and days at a time. The Town Center's managers were not sympathetic about our inability to make the rent on time. I tried and tried to negotiate all the way through the summer. By that time, however, I was missing payroll for our team members. Generally, people need to get paid, or they quit. And so, I had a lot of people quit in our Maryland location. And when people quit, you damn sure can't make your rent payments on time. At the end of the summer, The Town Center's manager stopped returning any of my phone calls, and hit me with an eviction notice. It was as simple (and painful) as that.

How did I feel? How did I feel? At first, I was in denial. I kept calling (and calling) management like a stalker ex babe. Maybe they didn't get the message? Maybe he just needs a bit more time to realize that we really belong together... Then, there is a point where your denial stops—like when you receive *the* actual eviction notice. And date to be gone. It's like the first time you see your ex out with someone else. It's real. It's over. But in my case, you really don't have time to feel or cry—you just have to act.

Just like when I moved out of the house, I focused forward, not back. I didn't have time to mourn my marriage or the loss of the salon. I stayed in "fix it" mode. If I broke down, what would my kids do? What would the team members do? I had too many people that were relying on me. Even if I wanted to quit or mourn or cry, it would have to be on another day. Today, there was too much to do. I will say that I did have loathing for the management. Why? I borrowed money from my mother's retirement to give them in good faith. They took it, but they still evicted me. I literally didn't have the energy to go clear out the space. Brian was a godsend. He transferred things that could be transferred to DC and the other stuff he put in storage. I never stepped foot in the Soul Maryland again.

. . .

Around July, I was contacted by a hair stylist looking for a new location to work in. She worked at a salon that I was very impressed with. In fact, I would consider the lady who owned the salon a friend. The stylist was unhappy with the owner and complaining about how unfair the working conditions and the salary structure that she was under were. She had heard about Soul, and really wanted to come bring her upscale clients to my ~~struggle~~ upscale business. I remember sitting in the car... Pause.

This is obviously a theme. I never had any privacy so it's no wonder that many life altering moments took place in my mobile office. I couldn't talk at home because of the kids or Daniel, and I couldn't talk at either of the salons. Thus, I was always thinking and strategizing and talking with the engine running with my cell phone on...in the car.

This day, I was talking to a friend and telling him how I was fearing the worst for Soul and that I really believed that we were going to have to close. But he was such an advocate for small businesses, he wasn't hearing any of that. He told me to do anything that I could to stay open, and that I was a hero, and I could make it work. Yadda, Yadda, Yadda. Aw hell! Just play to my little shriveled up ego, why don't cha? And that's really what I believed, too.

I had to believe it. I had to keep going and I thought that these new stylists (she wanted to bring another stylist with her) might be just the thing that would save Soul. I hated the fact that she was moving from my friend's salon. It felt like I was betraying a trusted colleague. But I was desperate! I didn't actively recruit the stylists, I thought, they came to me. I agreed to give them a higher percentage of commission PLUS (insert red flag here) pay for the assistants that they would bring. Now between the two of them, they had three assistants...At DC, we barely had one, and it worked out fine for the last eight years. No Bueno.

By the time they agreed to come over, Maryland Town Center had served me with the eviction notice. I had to convince the stylists to come to our DC location.

. . .

I never thought about the impact of mixing another salon's culture with our salon's culture. The two environments were very different. And all of the things that I did to get these two stylists to come over — i.e. create a salon boutique for one of the senior stylists versus being upstairs with all of the rest of them — probably left a horrible taste in the mouths of the other stylists.

Once the transition was complete, it was around October 2009. All the stylists and all the assistants were in there with the new customers. I remember being ecstatic! for about three minutes. However, one thing that I didn't factor in was the type of arrangements the stylists had with their assistants. At their home salon, the stylists made 45% commission and their own assistants. I offered them 55% commission (insert red flag here.) Plus, I'd verbally agreed (under duress) to pay for the assistants too. I remember October 31 like it was yesterday. I went over our numbers and I saw that it was the month that we had made the most in history of the salon; but it was also the month that we had the most expenses in the history of the salon. I had a big problem, and I didn't know how to undo it.

I went to the new stylists and told them about my situation. "Basically, guys I have over promised. I'm going under here—in spite of the additional revenue. I realize that I promised to pay for both of you at an increased rate and your assistants, but I can't keep up my end of the deal. We have two choices. You can pay for the assistants, we can get rid of the assistants, or we can reduce your commission. Well, I guess that's three choices."

Shenanigans ensued.

All holy hell breaks loose and I turned into Jay Z and throw the mic down at his *"Reasonable Doubt"* concert or something. Let me back up a bit...I came in the salon knowing that the two stylists were going to push back on the issue. One of the stylists said this doesn't seem fair, you promised, and on and on and on. And all I can remember was just being irate, and tired, and done. And I told them that they were ungrateful and did not know how a business should be run, or something like that and they pushed back and said that I needed to uphold my end of the deal. And I looked at them and said it's time for y'all to leave. If you do not want to continue to work here, you can go!

So they started packing up their stuff—huffing and puffing. And one of them went upstairs to where the other stylists were. Those ladies, who clearly heard all the commotion, were quiet and busily working on customers and were basically trying hard to stay out of grown folks' business. But then, one of the new stylists said *"that's why NO one likes working here!"* And that's when I lost it.

There was no violence, except for the words that erupted out of my mouth. I was done. All the anger and frustration from the loss of Maryland, from the loss of my marriage, from the loss of my house, all came out in that moment. What was I doing this for?!! From my perspective, I had put it all on the line. I worked another job to make payroll. I put my own needs and personal wants on the back burner to keep the business going. While Daniel and I definitely had our problems, the salon put an extreme amount of pressure into that cooker, too. In my mind, nobody had my back. All anybody cared about was the paycheck. And I get it. That is their primary concern.

But when they said *"that's why no one likes working here,"* I snapped. Freakin' lost it. Eight years' worth of snaps were lost. I looked around to everyone and yelled *"So y'all don't like working here? Lisa??? You don't like working here? Toya??? You don't like working here? Damn! That's why our people cain't have a got damn thing! That's why our businesses fail! It's because we have no loyalty! And so muthafuc%^ selfish! I'm working two jobs, lost my house, and got a divorce in part over this bullshit!!! What if I QUIT damn Soul Day Spa? Huh? What if I quit all y'all asses?! In fact, yeah! That sounds like a damn good ass idea!!! Bye!"*

And with that, I turned on my heels and walked down the stairs and got the hell up out of there. Not my proudest, most gracious or elegant moment, to be sure. But all my daggone mistakes culminated that day. And it wasn't their fault, really. The sobering truth is that according to the SBA, 80% of businesses fail within 18 months. This was but one story.

The shit storm was coming our way for some time now, just like the tornado in *The Wiz*--my favorite movie of all times. Ms. Diana was running after Toto, not even paying attention to the fact that it was Thanksgiving and that a storm was chasing her. Here, I was definitely Dorothy. Girl, you can't out run a tornado! In this case, my tornado was magnified by the fact that the United States was in the midst of the *"worst recession since the Great Depression,"* which caused clients to get laid off left and right.

Plus, the banks apparently went into witness protection programs, so I couldn't find a loan to save my life. And the loans I had were awful and damn near usury. I had a major setback in Maryland's location, and while I could have found more people to work at the DC salon, I was simply EXHAUSTED and angry and depressed and lonely and scared. I was very isolated and in my feelings about all of the stress that I was under. The phrase "it's lonely at the top" may be true, but its even lonelier at the bottom. I couldn't talk to people about the struggles—the daily, moment to moment, second to second, struggles I had. I was getting it from all ends. I was back in court with my new divorce and custody disputes. I was getting behind on bills with vendors. I was getting behind on my mortgage with the bank, who was the one that was supposed to help small businesses. As soon as I got behind on my mortgages, they called the loan. The end was coming.

. . .

During those last couple of weeks in December, I talked to two people who had not weighed in on what was going on—my father and one of my parents' best friends, Ricci (pronounced ris-SAY). Now, to be clear, I talked to my mother all day, every day, for my entire life. And she was my rock of support. I also had my girl, Noelle. She was a pit bull in a skirt, before anyone even heard of a Sarah Palin, so when I needed to vent or talk out one of the 7,409 problems I had, she was always there. But, while my mom and Noelle had solid advice and could hit me with the *"girl, don't take no mess from nobody,"* I needed the more analytical, non-emotional and practical voices in my tribe to confirm that I was in fact at the end of this storm.

My dad and I were really kindred spirits — our birthdays were just a few days apart, so there's that. But seriously, my dad was a level-headed man who had also been an entrepreneur before, and sadly, he too had to close his business. He had trusted some people he shouldn't have trusted to watch the money, and they watched it alright – they watched it walk right out the door...with them. Also, he was a small business and no loan opportunities existed in those pre-Costco days in the late 1970's. After the big box stores did come to play, with more toys at substantially lower prices, Dad had to pick up his games and go.

I think I had that memory in the back of my head as the reason I hung in there as long as I did with Soul. I wanted this to work sooo badly! I wanted the Cobers to be vindicated and successful as entrepreneurs. And we were, until we weren't. My gracious! I did NOT want to be a statistic!! I did not want to be a loser. So, I fought and fought and fought...everything. And Everybody. Until there was nothing or no one left. All the joy and enthusiasm Soul had given me was violently eviscerated from my memory.

My dad called me after my *"99 Problems"* day at Soul. Dad was the personification of E.F. Hutton. Remember those old school commercials about the stock brokerage firm? The tagline was legendary: *"When E.F. Hutton talks, people listen."* That was Andre. Andre was a hilarious, kindhearted, and cool ass dude. But our home knew that Andre didn't do drama. He didn't talk and re-talk about stressful things. His famous tagline, which he still repeats to this day, is: *"Hell, if that's all you got to worry about, you're doin' fine. Shoot, if anybody ever tells you I died of stress, you better call they ass a liar...."* But in between the jokes and the cool demeanor was a brilliant and practical man. *"Nicole."* He usually calls me *"Nic,"* so I braced myself for E.F. Hutton time. *"Yes, Daddy?"*

"I'm serious, now. I need you to close the salon. It's over. You've done a hell of a job, but now, it's over, honey." His voice cracked. My dad was the tough, yet sensitive soul in our family. My first teardrop for Soul fell. *"Now listen. Ricci is about to call you. We've been talking about it, and it's time to go."*

Now, Ricci was like my salon Godfather. His wife and my dad worked together in the Alameda County Courthouse after my dad closed the liquor store. They all had been friends ever since. Ricci was also, ironically and poetically, one of the Bay Area's legendary hair salon owners and master stylists. He always was the baddest man in the room. I bet if he weren't a hair stylist, he would've created the Panthers, I mused. He was a militant ~~trapped~~ blessed with the gift for cutting the perfect bob. And he was likely the only heterosexual stylist out there (just kidding).

He worked under the legends in the salon industry in his early days and went on to own one of the most famous salons in Oakland for years. My mom always wanted him to do her hair, but for the sake of their friendship (and his sanity), he always declined. Ricci called me and repeated my dad's directive, except with a bit more insight, colorful language and a hell of a lot more edge. *"Nicole, my darlin'...F%^& all them! Hair stylists make me sick! And I'm one of em!! They can kiss my ass!! I'm so angry, right now! Damn it!! Let me tell you. This industry is awful. Terrible!! They take good people and suck the life out of them. I was a stylist and a man, and baby girl, they forced me into a semi-retirement I was so stressed out.*

It's a cold, thankless industry. You tried to make it a class act, and you did. But, it's over. I'm just gonna say it. Your parents are so proud of you. They are, and Karen and I are too. But, you know I understand and I'm telling you, it's ok to quit. It's time."

I hung up the phone and sobbed. I was in my bedroom, on my knees, crying. You know the wailing that's so intense that your ribs bones ache? You know the 'Pandora's Box just flew open and all its contents bitch slapped you in the face' kind of pain? Those types of tears were falling hard. Finally, the anger and remorse that had built up within me for years broke like Katrina's dams and the flood ruined everything in her path.

. . .

Have you ever attended a wake for a family member who no one really cares for too much? Well, that's how the last days of Soul felt--quiet and extremely uncomfortable. Most of the stylists relocated to another salon, you guessed it, down the street. Kathy and Jett and one of the massage therapists stayed to finish the last few clients we had. I did see Lisa on her last day and what she said to me left me incredulous: *"You never talked to anybody!"* she cried with real tears.

"What are you talking about?" I was so confused.

"You never talked to anybody."

This was the single largest piece of evidence submitted that the team members and I were clearly ships passing in the night. She was right, I suppose. But I didn't talk much not because I was a stoic bitch or anything. I was just consumed and distracted with trying to keep everything afloat.

Also, I hoped that they knew my heart through my actions: I attended weddings and birthday parties and gave baby showers for my team. I knew and loved their children as my own. For example, when one of my team member's family lost their belongings in a fire, we had a small collection for the baby girls. Did I share the ups and the downs of the salon and when we needed to pull together? Yes, I did. Did I take money out of my family's home so that I could make payroll? Yes, I did.

And in that moment, in my self-absorbed moment, I thought: *"Who talked to me??" "Who asked me how I was doing??" "Who said, 'I'm so sorry for your losses, Nicole.'"* Hell, I don't think anyone even visited me in the hospital with Cole. (Thinking about it...nope. Nobody.) I'm sure that there are other sides to the story, but that's mine.

I was so in my head about how we would stay open that she was right, I probably didn't talk to everyone. I thought my actions would do my talking for me. I did not believe that I mistreated anyone or was a poor manager. I was just a manager...who was poor. I saw that the lack of communication created a huge wedge between me and the team that could not be mended. So in December 2009, Soul Day Spa died.

Could I have hired new team members? Could I have hired booth renters? Yes and yes. I was DONE, though. I had no support. I had no love. And I had no energy. But what I did have was two young boys from two failed marriages. One was entering high school soon and one was a toddler. They needed me far more than this place did. And I needed me, too. With that realization, I began the process of shutting the business down for good.

CHAPTER Thirty-One

The Shady Aftermath

When I left Daniel, I found myself facing my biggest fear—lack of financial security. I believe a big reason that people stay in relationships that are no longer working is because of this reality I was facing. After I left, I was still contracting as an attorney, but the businesses still generated enough money to make ends meet. After closing the salons that obviously dried up. Moreover, I would have periods where I could not find contracting work.

I remember those days with such paralyzing clarity. I would get up in the morning, fix the kids breakfast and lunch, drop off Jason at Kilmer and then haul ass across Falls Church to drop Cole off at St. Joseph's preschool. Then, I would park, walk across the street to the Catholic Church and just sit still.

I could not focus on even the next day. I just asked Him to make me strong enough to get through that day. I'd wake up to overdrawn accounts only to rush home to eviction notices on my door, which I expected — I just remember trying to get home before Jason got home off the bus so he wouldn't see it.

As the money would come in, I would find a way to pay "in order"...whatever was going to get turned off next. My personal low point was going in to complete paperwork to see if I would qualify for public assistance. I rationalized that this was exactly what it was for. I was a job creator and a W2 person for more than 25 years. That might have been true, but I was so self-loathing at the thought about where I was. [How do politicians actually believe that folks want to be on welfare? That moms like this feeling? I can only speak for myself—it's a demoralizing last step. Ultimately, I didn't get receive public assistance because I got a gig shortly after completing the application. But what about people that didn't have a law degree? What about folks that are in violent situations and rely on the income of their abuser? I just became that much more sensitive to others after my own application was completed. I'm sure other folks would feel that compassion too if they were in that situation. OK...spotlight OFF. Dragging the soapbox OFF the stage. Thx!]

As an aside, I was also a long standing member of a non-profit organization called, The Twelve Days of Christmas, Inc. It's a national organization and its mission is simple, clear and effective: We have two fundraisers annually and with the money that we raise, we go and purchase Christmas and back-to-school items for dozens of children and families in the area. We have purchased everything from clothes, back packs and calculators to Christmas trees, gift cards for dinners, and *American Girl* dolls.

I remember during this time, we had one of our monthly meetings. It was at the workplace of one of our members. And every one was sitting around an enormous conference table, like a scene out of some mob movie when the five families convene. Very established and accomplished women — physicians, attorneys, educators, you name it. This one meeting was so humbling for me because I remember being late on paying my $300 dues earlier in the year — I think I borrowed money from a friend. At this meeting, we were having a conversation about whether we should give gift cards generally or tell them that it was specifically about food. Or something. I couldn't focus on the conversation because of the noisy argument in my head. *"You don't deserve to even be here! Hell, you need to be one of the families you deliver to with your broke ass."*

My internal negative voice was so good, ghetto — and mean. I nibbled on my brownie, shrinking in my chair, slowly. I took a deep breath and tried to pay attention, but I remember feeling petrified. Irrationally so. I felt like I would be exposed, that I didn't belong. That my only value was my bank account. The days had me so fearful, shamed and alone, that I was ripe for any ray of sunlight, I think.

. . .

That ray turned out to be Terrence. Originally, I met Terrence back in 1992. I was a senior at Cal, and I got an internship to spend the summer in DC, working for the American Bar Association, Center on Children and the Law! Turning 21, in DC? Girlfriend, I was loving life! I met Terrence on an Omega Psi Phi fraternity boat cruise. My roommate Yolanda and I were the flyest thangs on the Potomac River that night, forreal!! I saw Terrence and he saw me. Now...I will say, that thang was sexy. You know the phrase "Sexual Chocolate"? Or tall dark and...handsome. No he was not handsome. Serious. He was serious. You know when a man can just stare you down without looking away, no smile, just undressing you with his eyeballs? Yep. Tall, Dark, Bald and Serious and Sexual. Yep. That was Terrence.

So it was like a scene out of some 90s Black love movie. I was standing, giggling with my gurl, sipping on a wine cooler wearing my navy blue and white polka dot flowing short set and white "bandeau" top courtesy of *Forever 21's* older sister, *Wet Seal*. Then Terrence gives me...the stare. You don't know if you are gonna get mauled or made love to! Lol! It was kind of intense, dangerous and smoldering. It's the thing bad boy legends are made of.

So the DJ had the summer hit *"They want Effects! Some Das Effects"* pumpin' hard. People started swarming the dance floor like roaches in the dark. He made his way across the room, took my hand, walked me on the dance floor and at first he just stood there looking me up and down. All this activity going on around us, like a scene out of *House Party* or something and he was just still. Then he put his hand on the lower part of my back and pulled me in close. Let the grind fest begin!

We were sweating for two hours straight, and at the end of the night I gave him the digits! But something was not quite right from what I remembered. He was really quiet and very...serious. While he was sexy on the dance floor, he was not much of a ....conversationalist. Extremely...serious. Uncomfortably so—especially for my happy go lucky self. We went out a couple of times, but nothing came out of it. It was fine though because I was in DC...turning 21 all summer long!

I went back home to California and graduated, but I decided to apply to law school. I came back to DC the next year and attended Howard, in large part because of the crazy amount of fun I had that summer...turning 21!

It turned out that I would see Terrence again. He was best friends with one of my law school classmates, Big Dawg Thomas. But again, I got the feeling that we didn't click—something just was not right. We never really talked a lot. Over the years, I got married and he got married. And Big Dawg got married, to one of my law school BFFs, Carla. Carla and Big Dawg moved to Philly and they settled down with their three! insanely gorgeous seeds (I really hate that word, but it's funny to write it and read it). So quite naturally between all her kids and all my marriages, we lost touch. Terrence and I would occasionally see each other at a kid's birthday party or two in the early days, but that was about it. Until Thanksgiving 2009.

. . .

After all those years, Carla reached out to me out of the blue. She wanted to come from Delaware to the spa to get her daughter, Kylie, who was turning 13, a manicure and pedicure for her birthday. I said great. We were pregnant with our oldest children at the same time. I remember the date she came down was November 20 because Kylie and my mom had the same birthday. So she came down and we got caught up on all the living that we had done over the years.

She asked me what I was doing for Thanksgiving. I really didn't have any plans as I was newly divorced and just an average cook. She invited me to come up there. I said *"Oh no, girl. I know you're being sweet, but that's OK. Maybe I'll take the boys to New York for the Macy's Thanksgiving Day parade or something."* *"Well Terrence and his kids—you know he got a divorce too? So they are coming up, so we will have tons of folks—you are more than welcome to join us girl. And my mom and..."* I didn't hear any more. Terrence P? The Terrence P that was Mr. Dancing Sexy man that I had known from way back? That Terrence P? Yes that Terrence P. Now, I didn't remember the serious Terrence...I remembered the sexy Terrence. When you are sad and stressed, your memory can be quite selective. Well the *"Ms. SpongeBob Hot-in-the-Pants"* voice in my head started thinking...*"Wow! Well maybe it wouldn't be so bad to be around friends and family for the holidays..."*

I reached out to Terrence and let him know that I might see him at Thanksgiving. He talked more in that two minute conversation then he did in the twenty years I'd known him! He seemed very genuine and happy that I was going to be there. Cool—it was definitely something exciting and would take me out of my impending drama that was going on in my own life.

The boys and I drove up to Carla and Big Dawg's house. And we had a great time! Carla and Big Dawg's three kids, my two and Terrence's two were all playing together and having a ball. And Terrence and I got...reacquainted. Well, I got drunk and he got drunk and so we got emotional. At about 3am we found ourselves in one of the kids' rooms, smooching and crying. Well at least I was. I was telling him about my disaster of a life and he was telling me how things hadn't gone as he planned either. But as the sun came up the next day, we were a couple. He was completely different from the old Terrence! Well, I didn't really know, but he was totally just what the doctor ordered at that point in my life.

From that point on we were in a very passionate love affair. He was obsessed with me, and I thought I was in love with him. Seriously, he was a different guy! We talked a lot about all our hurts and pains of the relationship mistakes. He listened and was my cheerleader. His game was strong for my impaired brain. I remember meeting him for lunch one day. I was going on and on about how I was a failure at business and relationships. He wasn't having it. I was awesome in his eyes. In his mind, we should have been married 20 years ago. *"Really?"* a little voice in me said. *"Cause you didn't talk at all"*..."*Be Quiet!*" Little Rose Colored Glasses Rosita shouted in my head. *"Let the man speak!"*

He said it wasn't my fault that those mutha f#chas (his words, not mine) didn't appreciate a diamond like me. I blushed. I was an amazing woman and he always admired me and should have followed after me, but I rejected him so...Rejected you? What? But you never said nothing...Rosita was glaring at me. I asked him if he had any reservations about me being married before, a very sore spot for me. His answer sealed the deal: *"Baby, those mutha fu#kas were just in my mutha f#ck'in way."* Word?! Hell, that was like the ghetto version of Billy Dee Williams saying to Lady Day Diana: *"Do you want my hand to fall off??"* in *"Lady Sings the Blues."* Well, at least in my mind it was. Little Rosita clapped, whistled and gave Terrence a damn standing ovation by that point. I was sprung. Terrence was my cheerleader and support system. Because I had a hell of a lot ahead of me to endure.

. . .

Were there red flags?? Well, anytime that you are in the middle of closing your business and receiving your divorce papers, that's probably not the best time to start a relationship. Then, there is also the fact that you're also considering bankruptcy. But, I honestly was not ready to face all that loss at that time, by myself. And Terrence was just what the doctor ordered. Some people do narcotics. Other people eat lots and lots of potato chips. I get into long-term committed relationships with the wrong dudes. But I didn't know that at the time. All I knew was the fairytale that I was telling myself was completely supported by the fairytale that Terrence was telling himself. We were made for each other! This was a twenty-year delayed love story that everybody bought into. And that love or passion was the fuel I desperately needed.

. . .

2010. Honestly, I wish I could put that year in a damn *"Etch a Sketch"*, shake it hella hard, and erase every little trace of it. In between having wonderful dinners with Terrence, I was trying to figure out how to file bankruptcy papers, by myself. How do bankruptcy attorneys make money? It's definitely not off of real broke folks, to be sure. *"How am I going to pay you when I can't keep my lights on?"* I was thinking as the Virginia bankruptcy attorney was telling me all his fees, in his $250 consultation meeting. Seriously? I drove my car down to Old Town Alexandria to a stately little old Bankruptcy court building. It sat on the corner of a very busy intersection of Old Town.

Crap, I thought. Of course, someone I know will see me, I'm sure of it. I parked my car right in front of the door, put my shades on, and ran in to pick up the papers to start the proceedings. To their credit, the administrative staff were very kind. They didn't make the awful situation worse by giving me the side eye or shaming me. That was a small present I needed or else I would have probably run out of there crying. The process was pretty straight forward. Just list everybody you owe money to, check. Then list all your assets — well that was laughably simple — NOTHING! That's why I'm here!! [To all of you that are deciding whether you should do this or not, call me. Especially if you have no assets. Get it over with so you can start the process of digging yourself out of it. The head in the sand approach NEVER works. I digress.] The hardest part of the entire process was the anxiety I had BEFORE I filed, honestly. What will people think? What will your credit look like? (Hell, once I opened my business, my credit was shot anyway.)

My anxiety, plus the stress of the calls from creditors were a beast! Yuck. Yuck and Yuck. They get some of the most aggressive people to bully you and it was a nightmare. I was cussing out complete strangers who were getting their rocks off by humiliating me. Not a great way to live. Once I filed Chapter 7, the calls stopped and I could exhale and try to heal. But you can't heal until you take care of the injury.

In addition to that, I was also trying to represent myself against The Town Center who was suing me because they evicted me for failure to pay timely rent. I think the amount of the litigation was about $709,000 that they were coming after me for. This was definitely a "Tums" relief time if ever there was one.

Further, my good air quote "friends" at the Bank and the Asset Finance Corporation were now my creditors. The happy days of Mr. Bobby's smiley face were gone. He wouldn't even return my calls now. They put another person on the phone and she had more aggression in her little baby toe than Mr. Bobby had in his entire body. They wanted to get the property back. So yeah, that too. The property that at one time was valued at $750,000 was now unsellable, by me at least, so the Bank and the Asset Finance Corporation got that property back. That's right, it went into foreclosure. I was trying to figure out all the options, but every route led back to bankruptcy: I could try to sell the property. But even if I did then it would go not to me, but to the bank, and the rest to the owners of The Town Center.

Once I made the Hobson's choice to close, I had to face my fears and have a liquidation sale of everything within the property just so I could pay some of the team members the money that I owed them. Terrence was my support system and pain-number. In order to shut down the operations that I had, I had to have some kind of focus. I remember all the things I had to do to close down my business that day.

Each room I walked into, I literally remembered the beginning of Soul. I remembered making every purchase. Every chandelier purchase. Every pillow. Every piece of art work. And now customers were getting them for a steal. What was even worse, there were several folks that showed up on closing day who never stepped foot in the spa to support me when I was in business. But, they would purchase my treasured artwork for a steal. Thanks!! That really hurt. It's interesting that she got this email but none of the others I sent in eight years of business, I muttered. Now was not the time for hurt feelings, girl, I thought. Just stop feeling and keep moving. It will be over soon.

Terrence and my brother on site to help customers move big items they purchased away in their cars. Terrence would give me a hug just randomly throughout the seemingly endless day. And that gave me the courage to hold my head up when people asked me why I was closing and what happened and all that.

And I did get through it. There was no way, even looking back with hindsight, that I could have done any of the things that I did without having some kind of support at the time. Terrence was my weed, coke, wine and double-cheeseburger all wrapped into one package. In Terrence's eyes, I was a strong and beautiful woman who could get through this. He was a beautiful distraction from all the pain in my life. He wrote songs for me. He was attentive and caring. He helped me literally leave my apartment occasionally and try to live a bit after closing the business.

There were days, no actually months, where I would have panic attacks about the thought of going to the mall or some public event. I thought old clients or team members would literally assault me for not being able to redeem a gift card or pay the balance of their checks, since we closed so quickly. He held my hand and my heart intact in 2010.

There is no need to disparage him (and face litigation) because for a marriage to dismantle within such a short amount of time, it's clear that we made a mistake from day one. We were great as boyfriend and girlfriend. But the pain that was within each of us was never addressed. There was no way in this life or the next that we should have ever gotten married. There were so many components of our relationship that were absent and issues we did not address honestly. We were two extremely emotional individuals, who made an impulsive decision to try to heal our broken hearts. And we failed miserably.

Terrence and I married and separated within six months. (Think Freda Payne *"Band of Gold"*). Terrence and I put Band-Aids on broken limbs thinking we would heal. He had a lifetime of wounds that he absolutely refused to acknowledge – or rather he believed that love could cure it all. I was his mirror image: I believed that the love and support we shared could take away the volcanic loss that I had just experienced in my life. Within one year, I had lost two businesses, my car was totaled, I got a divorce AND I filed for bankruptcy.

Instead of being in fetal position in a drug den, I was walking down another aisle in a rose-colored love high. And, as all addicts soon realize, the haze and high fades. You have to live. You have to address your fears. Is it a surprise to anyone that a marriage created to mask pain would not work? What tools did we have? What issues had we discussed? Now, the high wore off and we could not even have a full conversation within three months. That realization is painfully shameful to write, honestly. We also never spoke about how we were going to integrate our kids together. And Jason was now entering high school and facing challenges of his own.

To our credit, we did attend one marital counseling session. I'll say while it did not help us reconcile, it was life changing for me. I can't remember the counselor's name, but she left a very positive impression on me. She was an elegant, yet down to earth lady. I mused that she was older than me, not from her appearance necessarily, but because she shared that she was the mother of adult children and that left me, for whatever reason, feeling more comfortable. I was not a fan of counseling. I had tried it, ironically, only within the context of failed relationships. Apparently, I was always more concerned with fixing a relationship than fixing my own life (Aha! moment). Her office felt like what I imagined a womb would feel like: dimly lit, warm, toasty and quiet — minus all the moisture.

Anyway, when I say the joint session was a complete disaster, it was. I think it was the day before Father's Day. After the session, he took his kids, sans me and the boys, to Philly. As if the writing were not already on the wall, we separated a month later. Honestly, in the world of tabloid TV, I'm absolutely sure y'all want to know what happened. I challenge you though...Be better than that. I'm calling on your higher selves to do better. No, it was not pretty. And no couple is in their best light on the last day of their relationship. But I am thankful for that last day. Because that last day was the first day I asked myself a very important, life changing question: WHAT THE HELL IS WRONG WITH ME?

I could embellish here and say I cried uncontrollably when this happened. I did not. I was still numb and that was a problem. I couldn't talk to my BFF and my mom because they supported the breakup and felt that it was his fault. *"You did the right thing, girl!"*

"Keep it movin!" Riiight, I mused. But focusing on him being the problem wasn't honest enough. I was 50 percent the problem. And I wanted to fix my 50...cent. But where would I start?

PART Four
EXPAND.

CHAPTER Thirty-Two

The Runaway Bride...In Reverse

My mother has three anecdotes that she consistently recounts about me. She doesn't tell other people these cautionary tales. She only shared them over and over again with me throughout the years. She wisely retells them to me after I have suffered a reoccurring pain or failed to learn a lesson that has morphed its way through my life in the form of new situations or people. When she does this, it's never in a condescending manner. It's as if it comes to her as an epiphany, like *"Goodness, Nic! Do you see the lesson here, too?"* I am finally getting it!

. . .

"You Can Have All My Toys"
Story One:

When I was about 4 years old, my mom was cleaning up our cute lil home on Rawson Street in Oakland, California. As was her ritual every Saturday morning, she would put on a lil' cleaning music in the background, maybe the Spinners' *"Love Train"* or Al Green's *"Let's Stay Together"* and start cleaning that cute lil' home on Rawson Street from top to bottom. She took pride in it, as well as showed her baby how it was done. This day, however, was different. Usually, I would be right by her, with a baby doll in hand or my lil' broom or mop and I would pretend to emulate her efficient cleaning style. But again, today was different.

Mom said she heard a consistent noise, like a bump bump bump, drag, scoot, scoot! and then the screen door shut. She left the kitchen and went toward the front door, where the cacophony of sounds came from. There she saw a little girl, her little girl, carrying every one of her prized possessions — a baby doll, a rocking horse, and the new Sit n Spin she had just received for Christmas — all out the front door. Curiously, Mom stood quietly and watched the events. There stood her 4-year-old daughter, standing anxiously next to the entire pile of assets she had acquired in her tender years, as the older neighborhood children started gathering around. Then, to her surprise, Mom heard her daughter say in earnest: *"Please play with me. You can have all my toys!"* As the children started to motion toward all my worldly possessions like vultures to a carcass, my mother cussed every single one of those children out: *"Y'all go on back to your damn house. And leave my baby's things ALONE!"* They dispersed in an instant. She sighed deeply as mothers do when they ache at the pain their children's innocence's brings. Then, mom swiftly picked me up, putting me on her hip and miraculously carried all the toys back in the house with her free hand. I was a little frightened because I didn't understand what I had done wrong. I was giving to my friends. I wanted them to be happy. She looked at me in my big, Hershey's kiss colored eyes, gave me a firm kiss on my forehead and said sternly: *"Nic. Baby. You just can't give all your toys away for your friends to like you."* With a look of utter confusion in my eyes, she realized that it would be one of the most difficult lessons for her child to learn.

"NO BLACK MAN WILL WANT HER."
STORY TWO:

My eighth grade graduation was an amazing accomplishment for me. I got accepted to one of the best Catholic high schools in the Bay Area, I received awards for everything — Best GPA, Best Athlete, Most Spirited, blah, blah, blah. I was Class President, I think too, so I got to say a little speech during the ceremony. I knew this time was coming and as a part of my speech to the class, I memorized a poem, *"Don't Quit."* My entire family was there to hear that and to see how hard I worked. I was so happy, excited and proud.

My mom later told me about a conversation that she had with her mother on that day of pride for the entire family. My grandma smiled her Annie Mae smile and said to my mother, seemingly to crush her moment of pride: *"Bar-ba Jean, you gonna make it so that no Black man will want that little girl."* My mom was shocked and indignant. She replied: *"Well if a man can't accept a beautiful and talented and intelligent woman, then he doesn't deserve her, Mom!"* Maybe my mom was a bit of a revolutionary after all...

KINDERGARTEN LOVE.
STORY THREE:

By way of background, as you can now see, I have been what you call a "serial monogamist." I have always had a man or at least a man that consumed my mind and heart. In fact, my first "relationship" was literally in kindergarten. I remember it like it was yesterday. His name was "Allen." And Allen was a beautiful Hispanic looking version of "Fonzi" from *"Happy Days."* I don't know what his mom did to his hair, but every morning, he would have it gelled back so...cool-ly. But I don't think they had gel back then. Anyway, the hair and the Jacket! Oh that jacket was so...Ayyyyy!

Allen didn't really acknowledge my presence on a day to day basis, other than sit next to me on the carpet for circle time, but we still had a connection, I was sure of it. Then, one day, he missed a day of school because he was sick. Then another. And another. I. Was.

Devastated. I asked the teacher, Ms. Lojude, what happened to Allen. I think the chicken pox got my boy. I felt so bad for him. Home all alone. No one to play with or sing songs to. Naturally, I sprang into action. I had to help my man and let him know I cared. I copied down his address off an assignment that each child in the class completed, titled *"My Home."* On the top of the paper, we each drew a house. On the bottom of the paper, we carefully wrote our addresses down. I'm sure that innocent little assignment was not intended for 5 year old would be stalkers, but hey, your girl was focused. Operation: Florence Nightingale was in effect.

In actuality, all I did was write him a letter (damn girl, in kindergarten?!) saying that I missed him and I hoped he would get better. I asked my dad to bring me a stamp and envelope home. I put the note in the envelope and asked my mom to escort me to the nearest mailbox that weekend. A few weeks later, Allen's mom came to the school to specifically tell me that Allen said "thank you" for the note. Mission Accomplished! I remembered feeling slightly flushed in the face. But more than that, I felt that I did something important. Something that made my heart race. I made someone feel better. The endorphin rush was amazing, and it's a high that I've always associated with LOVE. In retrospect, I'm in utter shock (and slightly horrified) that at such a young age, I was so focused on love and expressing it without fear. But I do believe that you come into this world with the heart, mind and soul that the Lord meant for you to have to find your way through life. Thus, it was clear to me that one of my goals was to find love.

. . .

These stories were kind of triggered by my session with my nice little counselor lady. I still can't believe that I never went to a counselor for myself before. I decided to make my first personal appointment. It was really because I trusted her. She was the kind of figure that I liked the most: maternal, kind hearted, smart and helpful. It was a bit ironic that Terrence tried to block my insurance, which allowed me to get counseling. I asked her if I could come since we were separated. She said that's the time you probably need it the most. I was able to have six sessions. And those were probably the most productive six weeks of my life.

I talked about my childhood and how I really never had any problems until I got to DC. Some of those stories I told her were proof of two things: I've been a people pleaser since day one. And *"I've Got Love On My Mind"* by Natalie Cole should be my life's theme song. I felt like I was a pretty simple person with basic needs. How had my life become so complex? I just wanted her to help me understand myself. What was I afraid of? Maybe she could give me some insight and tools.

Public Service Announcement to Black People: Listen, Peeps. Counseling is a *good* thing. It is not a White thing. Trust me. I too was a bit skeptical: How could a complete stranger tell me anything that my momma and my BFF couldn't? I mean really? I love the episode in the new hit show, *"Blackish"* where Dre's mother, masterfully played by the actress that is the momma in all the Black movies...Jennifer...it will come to me....Lewis...mocked the wife Rainbow, played by the gracious, brilliant comedienne and fashion goddess, Tracee Ellis Ross, for going to counseling. *"Black folks don't NEED counseling! We have Jesus...and baths!"* Brilliant! Flawed and wholly damaging to the race's psyche, but brilliant — and accurately stated. I will not scoot the soapbox out BUT, this has got to change. I think the only "therapist" our folks trust is Iyanla and Ms. O, from the comfort of their homes. The perception that something is wrong in the head is sooo scary. But for me, I just wanna know, grow and GO! I don't want to be beating my head up against the wall forever.

Also, you might be able to lie to yourself after one divorce...MAYbe two...but girlfriend, have several seats after three. It's...not normal! Ok, I could admit that to myself, and I wanted to understand why it was happening so...let me just share my experience with the little cool lady, and you tell me what you think, mmkay?

I think there were a couple of revelations, takeaways, if you will, from those sessions. First, I thought she'd be all judgy about my relationships and tell me that I had some defective or recessive gene that caused me to be a relationship addict. She didn't. She noted, and that's really how I saw it, that I was basically a loving person, a caring person who should try to focus more of that love and care on myself. Gee, lady. It was a little disappointing, initially. Self. Love. Riiiight. I remember when she said that, it produced a bit of anxiety in me. To me, "self-love" meant being BY...MYSELF. But I like people. Well...in small doses. Actually, at that time I liked a few people a whole lot. They were reliable, and I could trust them. I was never a big group people person. I like REAL folks, which explained, in part, why relationships were a comfort zone for me. But I'm getting ahead of myself here.

I asked her what did that really, really mean. How would I know if I "loved myself"? I mean, I can't "hug" myself. I can't write myself love letters. I'm not being sarcastic (well kind of) but I just felt like I did love myself, but I was obviously focused on other people...a lot. And that was her point. She asked me what did I enjoy? I said...helping other people. And then, I cried. A real "plaintive wail"... (A pop culture aside: I remember that phrase from the OJ Simpson trial...remember someone said that it was a particular time that Nicole Brown Simpson died because they checked their clock when they heard her dog's plaintive wail. I looked it up...very mournful...sad...pitiful sound. What an interesting phrase, I mused. I have incorporated that phrase into my peculiar vocabulary ever since. Sorry for the tangent!) I was so...plaintive...because I didn't have a freakin' clue what I specifically liked except making other people happy. How pathetic.

I told her I felt like Julia Roberts in *"The Runaway Bride"* except...in reverse. In the movie, there was a scene where Richard Gere, who plays a reporter, tries to crack her code...i.e. figure out WTF is wrong with her. She too was so nice and pretty and smart and relationship oriented. Just randomly one day, he asked her what kind of eggs she liked. He had interviewed her previous fiancées and asked each one that question: *"What type of eggs do you like?"* Each of them said something different: fried, scrambled, sunny side up. What was interesting though, was that they each said how much Julia loved that kind of egg too! Well how could this be, Richard challenged a confused Julia. NO one can LOVE three types of eggs! You don't know what the hell you love, girl, he said (or something like that). You just love making those foolios happy and then you are happy! She looked incredulously at him. It's time, he said in summation, to find out what kind of eggs you like, ~~Julia~~ Nicole!

When my counselor said that it was time to find out what I truly like, my similarities with the runaway bride (in reverse) really hit me. Happiness for me was always a two-step process. And that process was as follows: I do something to make someone ELSE happy (i.e. get good grades, like basketball, go out partying, etc.); then they would BE happy (temporarily); they would say something nice to me, and then my happiness could be released from its shackles. NOT. COOL.

I was always trying so hard, but I never put that effort into understanding what I fundamentally liked. If my happiness was always rooted in someone's authority and control, it rendered me powerless. I really never looked at it that way. As controlling as I can admittedly be, that conclusion baffled and strengthened me simultaneously. At a minimum, I wanted to be in control of...me. I think I was so focused on the man or the external situations that I failed to focus on me. And the results were disastrous. And so, with my counselor's encouragement, I set out, alone for the first time in my life, to figure out what I liked and how to do loving things for myself.

CHAPTER Thirty-Three

"Wake Up!!!" —Radio Raheem, "Do the Right Thing"

After that counseling session, I can't say that I immediately sprung into action, like a *Rocky* movie music montage or anything. I think that I went back to doing what I always did which was...trying to find a job. Work was always my comfort zone. Accomplishment was my comfort zone. I guess you could say I'm a goal-a-holic, which is different from a workaholic. Goals are a very specific type of work, right? I'm working toward something. Whether that be graduating from 8th grade with honors or passing the California Bar or getting married or opening a business. My energy and work product all lasers in on a specific thing to do.

I think I've been like this since I was a child. My mom says as early as kindergarten, I was goal oriented. Teachers would say at my parent/teacher conferences, *"She's so mature and focused."* It's true. For example, I loved cursive writing. Still do. I have an early memory of being about 6 or 7 and jumping up in the morning, rising and shining, looking for a piece of paper to practice my cursive. Not going to the bathroom, or eating or brushing my teeth, but practicing penmanship.

Further, when I was in the seventh grade, I remembered contemplating what I was going to do *after* high school...during my recess. Now, do you understand I hadn't even applied to high school yet? But I was already panicking about what my life would look like after I got out of high school. It hit me that I had to get great grades, I had to go to a great high school and college, and I had a flash about being an attorney. But to be an attorney, I had to do all these other things first. Maybe that was my first bout with true anxiety. The panicking sensation of wondering what was I going to do. From that day in the seventh grade until the time after Soul closed, I believe I was in an extended anxiety state or adrenaline high. I just didn't know it. Anxiety makes me highly productive. I think going to my first counseling session helped me reflect on this a bit.

For the first time, however, I didn't have a career goal. I didn't have a vision. I didn't hope for anything except being able to pay my rent. And that felt uncomfortable at first. In terms of work, I landed an extended contract job that lasted for more than a year.

Now, I've never taken the time to describe exactly what being a temporary attorney looks and feels like. From my perspective, I always thought it was a wonderful safety net. I was always so grateful that I could make a living and care for my kids without the demanding responsibilities, the stressful hours, etc. The challenge, however, is that it was temporary. Most projects would only last one to two months, tops. This one was different. I got on a contract for nearly a year and a half. I had great flexibility. And great people who I worked with. It was a small group of about seven or eight attorneys. Typically, contract land or Temp Town is the place where the law (and some good attorneys) go to die.

What do I mean by that? Well, as in life, there is a pecking order in the legal profession. A totem pole of talent. A hierarchy. And when you are in contract land, you are arguably the lowest person on the proverbial pole. The partners and associates at the law firm know it. The managers on the projects know it, and exert their faux power whenever they like. They seem to like busting your chops here and there, like the 15 year old fry manager savant at *Wendy's*. But most significantly and painfully, the contract attorneys undoubtedly feel it. Most attorneys who are in Temp Town, most assuredly, do not want to be in Temp Town.

No, I take that back. You have different categories of temporary attorneys. First, you have those like myself. I had worked at a large firm, so I didn't feel — inadequate or less than. Also, I was (or used to be) a small business owner, and there were many attorneys like me who had their own thing on the side and contracted to make ends meet. Then, there were the others, who could not leave Temp Town. Some people had higher hopes, and wanted to be an associate or partner at the firm. For whatever reason, that didn't work out, and there was a lot of resentment in the air. I personally believe that there are people that are wildly intelligent, but there are only so many spots at the top, you know? It's a very elitist profession to begin with. The general public looks at lawyers on TV and believes that you're in court all day and that you're making hundreds of thousands of dollars. What you're doing, in reality, is creating hundreds and thousands of dollars...of school debt. But they don't tell you that during the application process. So you have a lot of people with a lot of intellect, but not enough slots at the top to utilize their talents. That breeds a lot of resentment and frustration. And a lot of people turn to contracting to not only make ends meet, but to pay off the massive debt that they've accumulated. But, again, I digress.

While I was grateful that I had a long-term temporary assignment, I was aggressively trying to find a real goal/career/meaning of life full-time job. After all, that was the zone I felt most empowered in. I've always been successful professionally. But at this time, nothing was sticking. I updated my resume and added the fact that I was a former CEO for a chain of small businesses. The description category was chockfull of goodies: managed a staff of thirty team members; drafted my own employment documents; registered my own trademarks; developed my own marketing and press campaigns.

This all sounds like good stuff, I thought. Wouldn't a natural transition be to apply to other hospitality related businesses? I thought so too, but no hits. OK, what about human resource management positions? Again, I signed up for applications online. No hits here either. Now I was starting to get a little nervous. I didn't want to go back to being an attorney, but then I started putting in applications for law firms, both small and large. Still...no...hits.

Now that's when my anxiety started to rise again. What about USA jobs.gov? I'm in the land of the government, surely they could find a place for me? I sent out tons of applications on the website. No return phone calls. At this point, I just start looking for anything. I even looked at an insurance brokerage firm. I hated insurance, and I hated sales, but I went to a job fair... A career fair...at a Radisson or Motel 6 or something (pride comes before the fall, right?). They took my resume and asked for a follow up. Then there was a round of several interviews where everyone thought I was great. But then the managing partner was like: *"Are you sure you want to work here??"* Good grief.

I know I put out more than 100 resumes over the course of a couple of months. I also "networked" and took people to lunch to see if they had any positions. Nada. I could not believe it! I had all of this practical experience from owning a business for almost a decade, but I could not *pay* for an interview after Soul.

It was the most perplexing thing. And a demoralizing thing. All my confidence over my entire life was built around professional successes. That was my ace, and as an occasional, yet enthusiastic spades player, I always led with my ace. But at this time, I just could not find anything. I remember going out to an event one evening, and I ran into an old friend. Her name was Natalie, and she was a psychologist and just an all-around cool person. We connected through her brother who used to clerk with me for the judge. When I owned Soul, she was also an artist on the side and outfitted my salon with some of the most amazing abstract art I'd ever seen. So when I ran into Natalie, I gave her a big hug and she asked how I was doing. She obviously knew that I had closed the salon and respectfully treaded lightly on the subject. *"Fine, I guess?"*

I knew in the back of my mind that she would have a deep thought or two for me. *"Girl, I just don't get it. I've been an attorney at a top law firm, clerked for a judge and owned and operated two small businesses for a long period of time. But I cannot pay someone to give me an interview. I'm so frustrated. I'm not doing anything, and I'm scared."* And she said words that were really life-changing, when I think back on it. *"Well,"* she said, quite matter-of-factly, *"Maybe right now, you're not SUPPOSED to be doing anything. You've gone through a lot with the salon. Maybe now it's just a time to BE."*

The fictitious lightbulb went on over my head. In that very moment, my shoulders went down a little bit, and the knot in my stomach subsided. And I had a genuine smile on my face for the first time in a while. It was the closest I've ever been to relaxing in a looong time. I got it. And what she said was really in sync with what the counselor was talking about too, I thought. Just being.

Admittedly, I didn't know how to do that naturally. I was always doing, and not just doing something, but doing a LOT of things. Maybe it was my time to just learn how to BE, and possibly to heal. I was open. I was finally open.

CHAPTER Thirty-Four

"Believe In Yourself As I Believe In You." — Glynda the Good Witch, The Wiz

So here I was...ALONE. Alone. aloooone. I had no relationship to work on or improve...except the one with myself! Hello!? That was about the only full time job I had not applied for, until now. Lol! Also, I didn't have to work...at work. Contracting is a pretty straightforward, punch in and punch out, type of job. Dare I diss my colleagues and say...mindless. I called it, affectionately, my potted plant gig. As long as I was in my seat at the allocated time, I was pretty much assured a check.

That left me with A LOT of...downtime. And downtime...terrified me. I really didn't know why. Maybe it's because when it's quiet and you're still, whatever you're running from catches up with you in your thoughts. Whatever thoughts of inadequacy or loneliness you have can't be drowned out by anything.

In some areas, I was extremely proficient at facing my fears, but in other areas I wasn't. With my smaller fears, like public speaking, I would just force myself to do it. But bigger fears like being "alone" or not feeling like I was enough—I pushed those bad boys on the back burner. I would find some large scale goal to occupy my time, and my mind. Now, with no distractions, I just had to do the work.

I observed what was going on around me. I got to take inventory of my life. I got to look around at my children. I got to look around at me. What do I like? What makes me laugh? What makes me happy? What makes me healthy? I didn't even know. Personally, I never had gone to the doctor for any kind of well visit since Cole was born. So I decided before I was technically booted off the insurance, I was going for a physical. And everything looked fine, except I was borderline pre-diabetic. What the hell? Aw hell naw! Now, I have a lot of shit wrong with me in terms of relationships and credit, but I can always rely on a good heart and average cholesterol level to balance me out. And now I had..."the sugar"? Yes, folks referred to diabetes, a very serious disease, as..."the sugar." Listen, other people eat too much, do drugs, or drink. My two vices are dating the wrong men and sugar. In that order. Maybe in the reverse order now as I was almost pre-diabetic.

How the hell did that happen? Well, after I closed Soul, I got a desk job. Sitting for eight to ten hours a day. When I was at Soul, I was moving twenty four hours a day. And even though I put myself on the *Five Guys* diet, (not eating all day because I was running around but would run into *Five Guys* for a late afternoon "snack" period) I never gained too much weight and my numbers were OK. Or so I thought. But once I sat all day, all that went to hell in a handbasket. Well, that was indeed the jolt that I needed because out of all my damn problems, I was not adding a health risk to that list. I refused.

One day I walked into *Crunch Fitness* and bought a membership. I liked the fact that they had lots of cool aerobic classes that I could take. I didn't want to get bored. And this was really a significant accomplishment because I hadn't been in a gym in more than ten years. The last time I joined a gym was *Bally's* when I was working at the law firm. And they jacked up my credit so bad after one missed payment that I never went back.

I guess you could call me getting my health together my first act of love...self-love. People rolled their eyes when I said that I was pre-diabetic. They were just so surprised because I was not overweight. Note to file people: Just because you're not overweight does not mean that your heart is tight or your cholesterol is low or your sugar is regular. All of those things can go on in the form of a small frame. Trust and believe me I know what I'm talking about. I lived it. [Sliding the soapbox back off the stage.] I cut out my wine and my cupcakes and replaced them with...green things. I was OK with spinach, I guess, so I filled up on ChopT salads at first, until I saw that those suckers were getting like $100 a week out of me for stuff I could chop my own damn self.

So I did that. And then I made a regular appointment to go to the gym every day. And I really enjoyed it. There were two instructors who were awesome, Arthur the spin doctor and the Zumba instructor, Shana. They really got me fired up and ready to go. So corny, but it's true. I really became a gym rat for several months and on my next visit to the doctor, I was no longer in the danger zone of being pre-diabetic! That felt awesome. And ironically (well no, it's not ironic actually, it's quite literal) I felt better. And that tends to happen when you don't eat sugar every day and you move around. Surprise, surprise. (There's sarcasm floating all around that sentence, ladies.)

In addition to going to the gym regularly, I was still going to my counseling sessions. And at work, on breaks, I would be browsing the Internet for interesting news etc. I was an Internet-aholic, OK? Just looking for little affirming stories and messages. And that's what led me to seeing Oprah's interview with Brené Brown. It was a YouTube clip. Not more than three to five minutes. But it sucked me in. Dr. Brown was talking about her book and talking about how to live a wholehearted life. Interesting, I thought.

CHAPTER Thirty-Five

Super Soul Sundays and Myself

When I started working out, I really did feel better. I enjoyed dancing. I enjoyed meeting new people and connecting. And I'm very goal oriented, so having the goal of not being pre-diabetic was a win-win. I also realized that my life was less stressful. That was probably the biggest moment for me. It was the first time that my mind wasn't racing about a problem. I wasn't worrying about where I was going to get the money for payroll. I wasn't worried about whether somebody was going to quit during the holiday season. I wasn't worried or stressed about the IRS. I wasn't worried or stressed about... living. Another epiphany? It hit me after a few months. Although I was a bit lonely at first, I realized that for the first time in my life I hadn't been in a relationship, and there was an upside to that. I resisted being alone for so long because it was unfamiliar. Think about it: I had a love interest of some sort since I was...6! I was definitely what you call a trapeze love artist. In order to get over one relationship, I would find another ~~host to feed on~~ love.

Sigh, it was true. I was so afraid of the lonely feeling that I would just jump into another relationship to feel something. And obviously, when you enter into another relationship, it's because it makes you feel good, for a moment. That dude is sweet on you, and he's doing everything to get you, and you are in your euphoria. But then, the real person shows up, and that's where the work begins.

Since I never wanted to be alone, I worked extremely hard at making those relationships work, even when my Spidey senses (my spirit) were telling me otherwise. The fear of being alone was so paralyzing that I thought any relationship was better than none. For the first time, however, I realized that it wasn't true. I was actually, OK. That was the first step. I realized that all the drama I created in my life was about me trying to maintain relationships with people who weren't a good fit for me. I always presumed that being by myself was going to be painful. Therefore, I never let it happen. Now that I made a pact with myself that I was not going to get in a relationship, I realized that hey! this doesn't suck. I really faced my fear head on with that. And, I found that not only did it *not* suck, the opposite was true. It was actually very nice and peaceful. I realized that by letting some of the biggest stressors in my life go, that was my second act of self-love.

. . .

Self-love was always a concept that I struggled with. Now, I'm not self-loathing, but I would not take care of myself as well as I should have. I would always roll my eyes when my mom would say, after an argument with a husband or struggling to make something untenable work: *"Nicole, you got a love yourself just a little bit more."* What the hell does that mean?! I didn't yell at her or anything, but it was really a concept that was foreign to me. Self-love? I remember early on in my relationship with Daniel, I would pick up books about self-love and co-dependency and stuff like that, but I was not in a place to even understand what those things really meant. Of course I loved myself, I thought, but I can't hug myself. I can't give myself a smooch. That sounds dumb and frustrating. But after talking to my counselor, I realized a very simple principle: Loving myself or self-love meant that I did things that were consistent with taking care of myself, making myself happy, or consistent with peace.

Before, I would do things for other people and hope that they, in turn, would love me, give me affection or affirm me. And that made love a two-step process for me. Now, some of the changes I made in my life by removing big stressful situations or relationships were gigantic acts of self-love. Then, starting to take care of my health and my emotions and making myself a priority were also acts of self-love.

I think that's when the light bulb truly went on. I was starting to get it. And I think the only way that I really understood it or came to appreciate what was happening was because there was a demonstrative difference in how I was feeling day after day. I wasn't worried or in a constant state of panic or overthought, you know? Before, I had a very active mind and had lots and lots of responsibility. And I had been battling stress on two fronts, both in my home life and professionally. So when those active stressors were removed, there was a bit of space. There was a bit of stillness. And I started to recognize it, identify it, and want more of it.

. . .

I've always practiced yoga. Bikram yoga was a big thing for me. And that's when I first started to appreciate my quiet time. I did Bikram while I had Soul, and in those moments, I did get some quiet time. But as soon as the session would end, I could not find that peace again, which is supposed to be the entire point of yoga. But now that all of those relationships and business problems were behind me, when I did the yoga, I felt a deeper sense of quiet and stillness. And it felt exceptionally good.

I think this is around the time where I was so open to feeling better that I started looking for all kinds of things that made me happy. Also, I wanted to actively deepen my relationship with God. I went from church to church to church (literally) trying to find a good fit for me and the boys. We went to mega churches, and to mid-sized churches. However, we came full-circle when we came back to our tiny in size but huge in heart church around the corner from our house, First Baptist Church of Chester. The boys were the ones that requested it. We had been there on and off since Cole was born, and every time we went, whether it was once a year or once a month, it felt like we were coming home. Jason had joined the church when he was in fourth grade. So that was one very enriching thing that opened the door toward me renewing my relationship with God.

But interestingly enough, I think Oprah Winfrey and her peeps were the biggest catalyst for my deeper walk with God. It's true. It may sound corny. But, while I was surfing the net at work and looking for different things, I would look at little snippets of Oprah's show called *"Super Soul Sunday."* And she would have really big spiritual leaders on such as TD Jakes, Iyanla Vanzant, Marianne Williamson, Joel Osteen, Eckhart Tolle, Deepak Chopra and Brené Brown. Before, I had rarely watched Oprah Winfrey when she was on ABC because I was at work. Now, I'd see little snippets online, and it inspired me to look at the Sunday shows. I was so open to learning more about myself and learning to love myself a little bit more that I was drawn to what I heard. And the concepts that they introduced into my life were like jigsaw puzzle pieces fitting together. Each person came from a different background, a different vantage point of faith, and had a different personality. But they all sang in chorus, and had one universal message: God. Loves. ME. He loves me without condition. He loves me just for being me. I didn't have to do anything for His love.

And here I was, jumping through all these hoops my entire life to receive approval, affirmation, and acceptance from other people. When the One who made the trees and the solar system and the birds and ME gave me those gifts without condition. I just had to receive them. I loved that it hit me so hard and so forcefully. In fact, there was an article that I read where Oprah was interviewing Maya Angelou — one of her last interviews before she passed away. Dr. Angelou talked about the moment that she had that revelation — that God loves her. It made her weep with joy as she repeated it over and over and over again: God loves Me. God loves Me! And hearing all these different spiritual leaders say that one universal message week after week after week was a spiritual breakthrough for me. It was an awakening.

Another big lesson for me: Love cannot exist in the same space as shame. Dr. Brené Brown did a study on the concept of shame, and she talked about how lethal shame is in our lives. She said that shame prevents us from living a wholehearted life. At the core of shame is the feeling that we are not...enough. Not Good enough. Not Smart enough. Not Pretty enough. Not Thin enough. Not Wealthy enough. Not White enough. And if you don't feel like you are enough, that's the level where self-love is eluding you. You will go through great lengths to be considered enough. That made complete sense to me.

In my life, I guess since I arrived in DC, there were a few things that made me feel like I wasn't enough. I didn't feel like I was smart enough. I kind of felt like a fraud. I mean it started way back in high school. When I got into Cal. Did I really DESERVE to go there? You know the affirmative action hate lodges in your head. So even after graduating in four years with double majors, I still wondered if I really was good enough. And the same thoughts followed me to Howard University Law, my clerkship and to the law firm. It was so subversive.

And then, on the personal side, I had the relationship failures. The shame I felt was like a landfill corroding my spirit. How could I be a good enough mom if I weren't married? My boys needed a unit. I'm not enough by myself. Those were the thoughts. But once I started on my new journey, I had some strong tools to combat the shame and the false beliefs about myself. That's why the revelation of understanding and accessing God's unconditional love for me was so transformative. To Him, I was already ENOUGH. To Him, I was awesome. He created me. And His GRACE was the ultimate blessing to me. Look at all I had been through. Look at all the mistakes that I made. And He didn't leave me. He didn't shame me. I felt His presence now more than ever. I figured if God loves me without condition, then what is there to be ashamed of? Why would I focus on all of my shortcomings when God accepts me for who I am? And if the maker of all that is and will ever be, not only loves me but accepts me, that one singular thing gave me the confidence to love myself instead of shaming myself for my mistakes in my life. I realized that God was not in the shaming business. He is love. He is supportive and encouraging.

What was that voice in my head with all this criticism, fear, doubt and shame? Well, I thought, if it ain't God, it must be... something else. And from that day forward, I made a promise to myself to pay attention when those negative thoughts were showing up for me. I would shine some light on it. And I would choose daily, moment to moment, between Faith and Fear.

I looked back over the huge red flag moments in my life that I've shared with you (and those that I've saved for myself.) They were almost unanimously fear-based decisions, right? Or based on the belief that I was not good enough. Exhibit A. Moving in with Daniel? Fear that I would lose my business. Exhibit B. The Town Center. Same thing. Exhibit C. Marriage 1, 2, AND 3. Fear of being alone, fear of not being enough of a parent for my children, and fear of not being "enough" if I wasn't married. Good gracious. It was all making sense now. Those were all voids that I was seeking to fill — with marriage, with accomplishment. But now, I sincerely felt like God had sewn together my little broken heart together and filled my Soul.

On that day, my life changed. I really figured out the recipe for healing my soul: Love God. Love yourself. Love others. In that order. For so long, I loved others, tried to love myself, if the others loved me first. And God wasn't even in the equation, until I needed him, I hate to say. And that was just a recipe for disaster and unnecessary suffering. But what's so amazing about God is He never shamed me; He never blamed me; He was patient and waited for me to realize that He had been present all along. I think you have to sometimes have a dramatic and epic fall to truly and completely understand and appreciate the magnitude of God's grace.

Finally, the puzzle pieces all came together for me in the realization that while I could access God anytime, He was most present for me when I was experiencing "pure joy" moments in my life. Now this is where I get on my little soapbox. Sometimes I feel that religion clouds this particular point. There's a lot of shaming that goes on in religion. There's a lot of dogma and rules, and I think it's confusing to people. I also think that it's a distraction from accessing God personally and having a loving relationship with Him. I was kind of afraid of God. Especially growing up in the Catholic Church where all we really heard about was if you don't do something, you're going to be punished. You're not good enough if you do this, that or the other. And look ok, I really tried. I was a good girl and tried so intently on living my life within the lines. But when you think about it, Jesus died to absolve us of our sins right? All you have to do is except Jesus as your Savior and your sins are forgiven. I think religion clouds that very simple point.

And also, I don't think God excludes people who don't believe in Jesus. I don't know for sure either way. But guess what? I don't have to! That's above my pay grade. That's for God to determine. I just focus on the love and compassion parts. I think we focus so much on the rules that we miss the unconditional love and grace that God gives us. Ok, I'm off my soapbox again...

• • •

With this new realization and excitement, I started actively looking for my joy. I started looking for things that gave me pleasure for no real reason. And in those joyful, elated moments, I felt like me and God were having a play date. Seriously, it's true! His presence was palpable. For example, when I would go to my yoga classes and have that stillness and that quiet time with myself, I felt God's presence. Or when I started to volunteer at my youngest son's school. I would come and read books to his class and the kids were so engrossed in the books and how I'd use my funny voices to bring the characters to life. Afterwards, they would hug "Cole's mom" and I could see and feel the pride in Cole's face. God's presence radiated through me. When I would treat myself to a new cupcake at a new cupcake place and it had just the right amount of sugar in its frosting and moistness in its cake, I shared that experience with God too. Whether I was at an old-school hip-hop concert, or a wine festival, or meeting and reconnecting with friends, I focused on God and being in relationship with Him in those moments. I characterized these moments of "pure joy" as an example of how my relationship with God was deepening.

I felt His presence everywhere. And for the first time ever, I experienced authentic love. Real self-love and God's love, and I felt immense gratitude for being able to recognize it as such. I felt like He was saying to me: *"Hey lady. I've been here for you all the time. I'm so glad that you slowed down and realized that."* Before, I would just call on Him in times of fear or after the fact, matter-of-factly, to give thanks. Now however, I was looking for Him in all the small and the big moments of joy, and I believe I found an inner peace that had eluded me for a lifetime.

There's a song by Patti LaBelle called "*You Are My Friend.*" There's a line in the song that says: "*I've been looking around, and You were here all the time.*" I have no doubt that she's definitely talking about God. That song exemplifies everything that I realized in those moments. It felt amazing.

. . .

There are so many people who are afraid of being by themselves. Or afraid of being quiet and experiencing stillness. I know I was one of them. When you are fearful or feel like you are not enough, you use activity to distract yourself from your fears. It makes sense. It's like a kid who is afraid of the dark — he doesn't want those pesky monsters to come out of the closet. So instead of going to open the closet and seeing what's in there, if anything, he keeps the night light on. Similarly, we keep that night light on in our own lives. For some people, it's food, or nice clothes and cars or degrees or relationships. They are distractions not only from self-love, but more importantly, from God's love. Don't be afraid of the dark. You shouldn't be. Facing those fears sooner rather than later allows you to access the peace within. When I say I had to lose my Soul to find it, this is what I'm referring to. I had to remove all of the chaos and the noise and the dysfunction to truly experience self-love and peace. Ok, enough preaching, right? Things were really starting to come together at this point. I was stringing together one good moment after one good moment without a crisis. Those moments turned into days, and those days turned into months. I looked up, and I had one year go by, and I realized that I was rebuilding my life brick by brick. If I didn't say it before, I'll say it now. I deliberately shut off my attraction pheromones, meaning I was not looking for no man during this process.

Another point: people wonder why people like me marry over and over. Well, there are two parts to the equation. First, it's in our heads that marriage is positive, obviously. It's a goal, a very high achieving thing in our society, particularly for women, right? The media and cultures all around the globe support that formula. No matter how much money a woman has or how successful she is, somehow...she may not be enough if she is single. I totally struggled with that, as I shared with you.

But the second piece to this equation is men. Men love two things: women and a challenge. "Attractive" energy in a woman is key. Not exclusively physical, though men are absolutely physical creatures. And don't make the mistake of thinking that there is one mold for what's "attractive." For as many people there are in the world, that's how many versions of physical attractiveness that exist. It's all about the attractive energy. You can be fine as [insert actress name here], but if you have a negative energy, you will be a repellant no matter what. So to recap, if you have an "attractive," available woman, a man will sniff her out like the hound dogs in Mississippi my granddaddy had for years. I've always known the equation. I am that woman.

But when you are hurting from a failed relationship, and then shortly thereafter, an attractive man tells you how gorgeous you are, and how smart you are, and how he can make you smile again, tell me that doesn't have some power to heal? Especially if the woman is not ready to heal or deal. I know it, cause I did it. This was a first for me. I was the girl that was courting love in kindergarten, remember? I had to have that "love" feeling. But when I went for the feeling alone, it got me in a lot of trouble, right? I didn't want that temporary high anymore. I wanted to feel deeper love, so I looked at my scars and my own fears, and I faced them on some level. And by doing the work without a love "crutch," I had found the true source of my strength, which was outstanding. And the knowledge that I could face my fears with God as my source was very powerful. It stopped me from being constantly afraid of everything. I had been through everything and gotten to the other side — so what was there to be afraid of? My faith was even stronger. The gratitude I felt was immense. And so I slowly got over the shame of my businesses failing. I slowly got over the shame of my failed marriages. And I started to feel, not only better, but more empowered.

CHAPTER Thirty-Six

A Purpose Driven Life &
My Super Friends

Now that I had "my mind right," I felt ready to take another step. I started journaling about my experiences with Soul, and that was very therapeutic. But I also got the courage to ask God to give me a proverbial mitt, and put me back in the game. I wasn't afraid anymore. Well, honestly, I was, but the first step was that I was able to HOPE again. That was huge. And as my grandmother used to say, *"You have to give time, Time."* It was now the end of 2013. Soul had been closed for a few years. My final divorce was, final. My boys were really doing well.

Jason was in his sophomore year in high school. Admittedly, his freshman year was the worst. First, the drama of acclimating to Terrence's presence and immediate absence was a challenge. Also, he and his dad were now not even on speaking terms. Plus, at school, he had a disturbing incident with his English teacher. That foolio lady asked him, as the only Black child in the class, to read a Langston Hughes poem, *"Ballad of a Landlord"* quote unquote "Blacker." Yeah, you read that correctly. Not with more "emotion" or "feeling," but "Blacker." Now, this would have been bad from any teacher, but you mean to tell me an English teacher did not have one more word in her vocabularic arsenal than...Blacker? Now, look, I love colloquialisms even more than the next person, but she was wrong for that. If I need to explain why that was wrong (which I did, to the school board and to CNN), ok. But, it was a lesson that I had to teach my son. Needless to say, that incident put a damper on the freshman year experience. Finally, last but not least, I had him tested for ADHD that year as well. It was something I struggled with for many years. I didn't want to "label" him. I didn't want him taking medication. But I'll never forget that I was talking to my hairdresser Jana (remember her?) one Saturday at the salon. I told her that Jason was having a difficult first year. And she encouraged me to have an IEP assessment done on him. These are tests done to help determine whether a child might be eligible for Individualized Education Programs within the school system. She said, *"No child wants to fail, Nicole. I was just like him. I struggled. Have him tested, and if nothing is wrong, no harm. But if there is, there are all kinds of resources to assist him."* I trusted her. So I had him assessed. Shortly thereafter, I learned that a girlfriend's daughter had been diagnosed with ADHD and with the medication, her grades soared. She talked to me and was a tremendous resource for me. With that, Jason was properly assessed and treated and he felt so much better. By his sophomore year, his grades leaped to a 3.60 and that was while he was competing on both the football team and track team. That gave him (and me) such immense pride.

Cole's dad and I were trying to find our way as well. It was very up and down at first. But again we had to give time, time. By 2013, Daniel and I weren't communicating with all the venom and anger from the past couple of years. I think we had our first joint birthday party for Cole that year. I was grateful for that.

So with my personal life settling down on all fronts, I wanted to ask some bigger questions. I wanted to know my purpose. I wanted to look at what my value is to this world, and I wanted to be an active participant. I also was very grateful for God's love. And I wanted to go out and communicate to everyone in and through my gifts. What were those gifts? Well, I needed time to sort that out. But I started with a really great tool.

I picked up a book that my grandfather had given me 20 years before called *"A Purpose Driven Life."* The author was also featured on *Super Soul Sundays* coincidentally (I think not!). I'd never even taken a look at the book my grandfather gave me at my college graduation. But I carried from California to DC to Virginia with me, unopened. Now I was ready. I finally opened it. And it took me through the process of analyzing what my strengths were. What did I enjoy doing? What was I good at? And how can I be of service? It encouraged me to look back over what I did with Soul and how I put it together. I would write down the things that I enjoyed as well as the things that I absolutely hated. One of those things that I wrote down was I would not be adversarial. And that's something to say for an attorney, right? So one of the things I came up with was helping small businesses.

I also enjoyed the media. When I was in college, I always wanted to be a journalist, but fear held me back because I didn't think I'd be able to get a job. That's why I went to law school. On my new "Purpose" list, I put "journalism" down as something I wanted to accomplish. I also wanted to write a book about all of my experiences. Further, not only did I want to help small businesses, I wanted to speak publicly too. I really started to look at all the things that I had gone through. There was a lot of awesome stuff that I did. And I thought I could be a tremendous resource to other people. To show them what I did right, and to show them which routes not to go down. So I wrote that down as well. And I didn't rush the process, but I did write it down and I did ask God for his guidance. And I relaxed about it.

I had a girlfriend named Karen who was also an attorney. She was an executive business consultant. She and I met way back when I was preggers with Cole. She knew about Soul and had visited on occasion. Now she was really focused on doing everything she could to get her executive coaching firm to the next level. And she believed that I should absolutely be doing something similar. In fact, she invited me to volunteer at a women's empowerment conference with her around this time. She was so nice, and I was still a bit in my feelings about getting out there, but I said "why not"?

It was such a great experience because I could really see myself on that stage, maybe not that day, but someday soon. Again, I was believing and hoping once more. And, I was surrounding myself with people who believed in me and wanted my best too. By knowing how to treat myself well, I thought, maybe I'm attracting more positive people to me. Soon I would learn how right I was. Karen turned out to be one of my super-friends.

Another super-friend was Cara. Cara was my sister-in-law from Ex #1. She was a wonderful lady. I was still very close to both the boys' families. We kept in contact over the years, and I really valued their continued friendship, in spite of the divorces. Cara was a news anchor in the area. Though I had never told her this in the 15 years I'd known her, I really admired her. She was well respected, and I asked her for steps I could take to get some television experience. The first thing she did was "google" me. I gulped.

She was honest with me: *"Well, you have lots of various hits, but they don't tell a consistent story."* "Well," I said, *"what I'd like to do is use my experience to discuss small business issues."* She said, *"Nic—the people who appear on TV as experts have solid branding packages: websites, blogs, cover shots, other media hits, etc. Work on creating one, and then I'll review it. If it's good, I'll forward it on to our producer."* My God, I loved that girl! She gave me clear, specific advice and a goal. Basically, she told

me to *"get my shit together"* (she hates that I say that!),
but it felt great. I could have been discouraged that I
didn't have any of those things, but I was excited to learn
and put everything together, brick by brick. Karen was
so essential in this process. She was just ahead of me and
she shared all she had — photographer
recommendations; website developers; ideas for writing
articles; where to pitch for speaking engagements — all of
that! It was awesome. I remember still being in my
feelings a bit: what if I apply and no one responds? What
if I don't have enough speaking experience? But I just
applied anyway. I just pressed the "send" button
regardless.

The International Spa Association was the first
"yes" that I received! While I didn't have any of those
things when I applied, when they said they wanted to
see my "headshot" and website that was an even bigger
incentive to get my "package" together. I did, and they
approved me to be a speaker at their conference. Also,
Black Enterprise and *American Express* also responded in
the affirmative. It was beautiful. After a few months, my
package was complete! I took it back to Cara. She
reviewed it and was impressed. *"Nic—I think we are
ready, girl."* And I got my first shot in front of the
camera. Super-friend Number two.

And right around the corner, I would meet my
Superman.

CHAPTER Thirty-Seven

Mister Melody

"You are my melody, you're just as sweet as you can be, and it's good to know you're mine all the time." — Natalie Cole

I had a friend/colleague named Jeremy and Jeremy was an amazing graphic designer/brother that I had known for many years during my Soul days. Jeremy was my go to guy for all my beautiful marketing/PR/advertising needs. Flyers? Jeremy. Menu of Services? Jeremy. Ads in magazines? Jeremy. He was a friend as well. Whenever I was having a little relationship crisis and needed a male perspective, Jeremy was there. I remember many nights I would be closing the cash register for the night, full on preggers, and Jeremy would extend me a courtesy of delivering the flyers or whatever to me. I'd be a little teary or exhausted by all the crap I was going through, and he'd drop some cool, *The Secret*, Law-of-Attraction knowledge that I wasn't ready for at the time, but I still appreciated him.

Anyway, after the salon closed and he left his full-time gig, we reconnected because he was thinking about starting his own company called, *Graphic Life*. I would give him my thoughts and encourage him. One day, he told me he was meeting with two guys, Karl and Michael, who wanted to invest and be partners. I was suspicious, because, well, I'm always suspicious. And, Jeremy was a true ARTIST, so as his little lawyer sister, I just wanted to "check out" these dudes. He told me that they were meeting the following week and he wanted me to tag along. I agreed.

I drove out to Greenbelt, MD with a skeptical eye, but with really cute blue suede pumps on... (My style game had increased moderately over the years.) I really didn't know what to expect when I rode up the elevator to the 9th floor of this office building — I just wanted to help a friend get his business off the ground. I arrived at the office of Valley Real Estate Group, a respectable (and legitimate!) space. Sigh of relief. I knocked on the glass door and a gentleman came to the door and let me in.

"Hi, I'm here to see Jeremy Wood?"

The man looked clueless.

"Hi, I'm Andrew. You probably will need Michael, I'm thinking."

Oh yeah — one of the partners.

"That's right, thank you."

"He'll be in shortly — would you like to have a seat and wait for them to get here?"

"Absolutely! Thanks so much."

So me and my cute blue suede pumps, with a gold encased metal fronts (sorry) had a seat.

I waited for a few minutes...I was really into my new shoes, actually. I got a great deal, I was thinking, when in walked Michael, or as I would later call him, lil' Maxwell with glasses (which now causes him to appropriately roll his eyes on cue.) He was simply a beautiful man, and I don't give praise easily. Think Maxwell, the soul singer, circa BLACKsummers'night album. The clean-shaven, suave, so fresh and so clean, Maxwell. Michael had a slightly exotic look about him. How can I explain? Like, you know how some Black folks say, "I got Cherokee Indian (sic) in my family"? He really did. High cheek bones. Strong jawline. Wavy black hair with flecks of silver sprinkled throughout. And while he had cinnamon colored skin, the red undertones worked together to support a case that his Native American lineage was not too far in the past. Like a grandmamma or somethin', I mused. And this brotha was sharp! He brought a new meaning to the phrase "business casual." He had a light blue blazer on with dark pants and a button down, crisp white shirt and very nicely polished black shoes. Dang! I hate that I'm not more name brand savvy! Crap. Because right now I would be throwing out all the designer names here. Farragamo! Gucci! If not them, then somebody in Italy because the brotha LOOKED...foreign AND expensive. Seriously! Quite the impression was made.

But it was quick and brief. I remembered he had like a thousand books nestled uncomfortably underneath one arm and a cell phone in his other hand. As he walked in the door on the phone, he acknowledged me with a friendly head nod and smile but swiftly walked past me. I started to get up and greet him, but I was too late — he was GONE. Ooo.Kaay. I waited. Shortly thereafter, Jeremy walks in, to my relief. We hugged and he leads me through the reception area to a conference room where lil' Maxwell is now off the phone. *"Let's try this again,"* he says and greets me with a warm big smile and handshake. He apologized profusely and introduced himself.

Michael W. Adamson. MUCH better, dude, my lil alter ego judgmental Judy mused with her hand on her hips. He offered me and Jeremy seats. Just then, another gentleman walked in the door. Karl, the other partner. We all sat down at the long conference room table, each strategically placed at one of the four corners, like a compass, with Michael being "North" at the head. Jeremy started with the formalities as to why we were there and then everyone started with the introductions. Myself. Lawyer. Small biz interest. Love helping. Blah. Next. Then Jeremy. *Graphic Life.* His passion. Wants to rule the world through all aspects of design. Cool. Next! Karl Key. Residential construction owner. Former clothing designer with merchandise sold in retail stores around the country. Looking to break into a new business. Wants to have a graphic design company in portfolio. Cool.

And what about Mr. SpongeBob Busy Pants himself, Michael? Well Karl actually introduced Michael and all the while I was taking copious notes. I didn't look up. You could tell that Karl was proud of his colleague's/best friend's resume. Why wouldn't he be? With descriptive words like *"served on Board of Directors for the construction of the DC Convention Center," "former DC School Board member," "co-founder of Valley Real Estate Group"* and *"commercial broker and asset manager for more than $3 billion in real estate,"* I finally looked up from writing to see who did all that. I turned my head, due North to look in Michael's direction and was surprised by what I saw...a face of genuine humility and slight embarrassment. Those are characteristics that I find admirable; however, they are rendered extinct in the nation's capital. Cool. Cool. And Cool!

After a very long meeting, we agreed that they needed a partner that would come in and assist with the legal organization and operation of the company. I didn't have any real desires before I walked in the room, but I was so excited to be a part of a new company with partners who had their own strengths, that I said yes. And so, we got to work as the partners of *Graphic Life*.

My first impressions of Michael were really ones of respect. He was very cordial and respectful. And I never got...a vibe of interest. Not one. Definitely not from him. And for me? He was attractive, yes, but...nice and...not over 6 feet...and a Christian conservative. Like pastor-line kindness. Like nice for no reason at all, nice. Like church was a more than Sunday activity, nice, (I later found out it was.) Like, children's boy-scout troop leader for all 12 years his son was in school, nice. Ok, you get the point.

So, when I say this was N-O-T a love connection, it's true. Because I obviously didn't do straight nice with no drama guys, right? There was nothing on his resume that would ever take him out of the friend/brother category. The shallow three strikes against him? In no particular order: 1. I wasn't in a club, so there was no "chemistry"; 2. He was a nice, Christian boy (with lots of sense) and 3. He was height challenged [Sorry, this was a hard and fast criterion for me. Even though he was 5'10 and technically I *could* wear heels, at fast superficial glance, he was doomed by my shallowness. Yes, that decision was snap and made within 15 seconds of our initial handshake.]

Also, most importantly, I remember Jeremy saying in passing that he was going through a divorce or something and that he was having a hard time with it, but, I never got anything personally out of Maxwell. DRAMA. I thought. Lord, even if he was smart and Maxwell-gorgeous fine, and loved the Lord, and was an excellent and devoted father, he. ain't. ready! I told myself. He is gonna have to get RIGHT! Like ME! And love himself...blah, blah, blah. Not. Interested.

But, then I got to know him a bit better. Well over the months and months, I started to see Michael in a less hurried light. For one, it was clear that he was a really devoted dad. Outside of work, he was shuttling his 17 year old son to...basketball, boy-scouts and church, etc. Insert said activity here. Shoot, I thought. I was exhausted just listening to his schedule. He reminded me...of me! He also had two additional children — his daughter who was at a university in California, who he adored, and his oldest son, who was a college graduate and a senior citizen assisted living supervisor. Word?! He was a cool ass dad? You had me at #allkidsgrownandcollegeeducated. Judgmental Judy pursed her lips a bit.

I remember we went to *Silver Diner* for a bite for lunch. I think it was the first time he told me a bit about his life and how troubled he was that his marriage had ended, and how ending his marriage conflicted with his faith. I was uncomfortable. Not because of anything he did, but because I knew very well what it felt like to go through the end of a failed relationship. Plus, I didn't even think about the church folks aspect of the end of his marriage. He was really impacted by what was like a shunning by the church folks—they had been like his family for more than twenty years and with the divorce, it was over for him. Even though the divorce was as mutual as a divorce can be, he was now feeling divorced from not only his wife but from all the people who he had ministered and loved over the years. I had never dealt with that part. And I realized in that moment with my colleague that he really had lost a great deal more.

We were kind of like, friends. Like formal friends because we were sooo different. I was a California "liberal" (graduated from Berkeley, no less!) who was divorced 5,204 times. He was a native Washingtonian, Christian Conservative and a Black Republican (I'd never met one in my life. Gospel truth.), who had been devoted and in love with his ex-wife for 24 years. It was like being friends with...Mister Rogers. Seriously. Just imagine that for a moment. Mister Rogers...with a broken heart.

While there were differences, we focused on the one thing that we were in complete sync on...business! Man, that boy was bad! When he got in front of folks to talk about their business or their real estate or, most importantly, their money, he was masterful. He was a powerhouse. By the time he finished talking about whatever he was talking about, the proverbial *"panties would drop!"* (He hates when I say that.) In other words, deals would be made! Land would be developed! Money would be exchanged! I'd never seen anything like it! It was awesome. And we were a great team. I was a strong writer and organizer and he was a skilled orator and high level strategic planner. He had made millions before and was good at it. Me? Not so much. I was very small business, very mom and pop shop minded. He was a big picture, big business thinker. That was cool to see, I'll be honest....

After being frustrated with the dynamics of *Graphic Life* (i.e. we all did not work well together), Michael and I realized that we had lots more in common than we had thought at first glance. We decided to do our own thing. Something we really enjoyed was business consulting. *Graphic Life* was Jeremy's baby, after all. And we all had different paths we wanted to take. Michael really gave me the courage to believe in myself again, as a business owner.

At the time, that perplexed me. He didn't even know about my business. Why was he sooo confident that I would be good at it again?? But he said it over and over and (smile), I started to...hope and believe again. That was very cool. We developed a wonderful friendship and partnership, and that was a genuine first for me.

For him, I know that having a person who understood his divorce pains without judgment was very helpful. I can only imagine how isolating it must feel to be a part of something like a church and to have no real friends to support you when you "violate" the cardinal rule and get a divorce. I encouraged him to go to counseling, which was a total liberal thing to do, apparently. As was meditation (The horror!) He was very resistant to it at first, but as he began to trust me a bit more, and as I shared with him my process, I think he looked at me as a kind of divorce mentor who had gotten through to the other side with my sanity somewhat intact.

But the most important thing I encouraged him to do was to stop beating himself up. I was honest when I told him that he was a close 4th in the all-time great dudes' category (up there behind Jesus, Andre and Barack). And I'm very judgmental and critical, I said, so, he should (read *better*) believe me on that. I think I was the oddest little bird he had ever experienced in many ways.

And after the divorce, I even encouraged him to date. Yes, I did! (Even though I was honestly catching some internal feelings for him by then.) I knew that he needed some rebound booty, and while I wasn't it, there would be plenty of applicants in the DMV area waiting in line! At first, he gave me...crickets. Silence. Like yeah, whatever. Then, I think his boy Karl was talking about hanging out in California for something or another and...he didn't go. I think that's when I KNEW...and we have been partners ever since.

This "love thang" (in the words of The Whispers,) was not a spark! Not an overnight sensation. There was no dance floor, no loud music hypnotizing me in the background. In fact, half the songs I love from the 90s, he's never heard because he only listened to Christian music! Lol! It's the funniest thing to have him say, *"Now that is a great song! Who is singing it?"* I'm like *"Babe! That's Jon B, 'They Don't Know!' It came out in the 90s!"*

How was it to transition into a romantic relationship with him? I blush because we have all these kids between us, so I can't turn this into a Harlequin romance on ya. But I'll say that when you have a foundation of trust, complete trust in your love, it makes you less inhibited. That is an amazing feeling! In the past, I would use alcohol or music to make me relax. With Michael, I just needed his voice and words. I actually believe him when he tells me how beautiful I am or how good I look. And he wanted to please me, err um, make me happy, and that was very different in the intimacy area. (Is it getting hot in here?)

Also, I honestly had to learn how to be with a person that I didn't have drama with. I learned that I mistook the drama for "passion" or deep love. I had to really re-engineer my thinking about what love felt like. I never had a "break up and make up" pattern with Michael. That was different. He was a committed man that actually believed in the value of love and trust. I never was made to feel jealous or small or insecure. That was different, too. He actually made me feel like he adored me the way that I adored him! And that was very different...and passionate. We had mutual affection and care. And we could talk about anything.

His patience and maturity also grew me up...tremendously. In the beginning, when I would get in my feelings and raise my voice about an issue, he was not having it. He would look at me firmly but calmly and say, "Nicole, that doesn't work with me. I'm not like that. Just talk to me. I listen to you. I love you. I respect you. Just talk to me." Silence. It was as if Babyface had stepped out of a song and was having a conversation with me. Can you imagine raising your voice or having an argument with Babyface? Right. Me neither. (Or Maxwell...woohoo! If you haven't guessed by now, I have a Major crush on Maxwell and now I get to kiss his twin with glasses everyday! I'm WINNING!) Yes, this fella was indeed a different kind of brotha.

This love was born out of a quiet and serene place. I remember very clearly when I was open to the concept of dating again. After healing and truly understanding myself, I wrote a prayer request to God. I had never prayed for a man. Never. I just ran from some crisis or another, looked up our horoscopes, and gave it a go! (Insert cringe face here). But as my relationship with God expanded, I consulted Him and Him only. And this was my prayer: *"God, Please send me a person who embodies Your love for me."* I truly believe that Michael is that person.

Had I not gone through my period of "dating myself" or looking to truly love myself, I never would have appreciated Michael. I like to say: *"He loves me as much as I love me!"* Plus, he is a completely different kind of man than anyone I've ever been attracted to, and that in and of itself shows me the growth that I've gone through to get here. I was afraid and needy in each of my other relationships, so I attracted all the wrong types of people. They were not bad people, per se. They just were not the right people for me. When I started being kind to myself and looking to God and myself to supply my needs, I think it allowed room for Michael to walk in. We hear about the Law of Attraction, right? I believe that he is a very real example of it.

CHAPTER Thirty-Eight

My Life Now

2015 the **Magnificent.** That is what I will affectionately term the year when My. Stuff. Was. Together! And my gratitude is at a peak because I sincerely felt the depths of my lows in the past. That is why success is so much sweeter after failure.

I think the most important success for me was seeing both of my children soar on all fronts. Coley Bear, aged 8, was accepted into his school's Advanced Placement Program in the 3rd grade. Me, Daniel and Jason worked with him extensively in the 2nd grade on getting his application together. He did extra credit assignments. We advocated with his teachers and administrators to let them know we wanted him to apply. We worked together as a family to make sure he was getting the right grades. And he did it. He started the 3rd grade off with strong grades, so we know that this curriculum was the right one for him. I love seeing how he and his father are working together on his academics and his little confidence is building. Very cool.

With regard to Daniel and me, I think the best compliment we've received was at Cole's first parent/teacher conference. His third grade teacher, Mrs. Tope said, *"Can I just tell you how much I love your son??! He is so sweet, I just want to take him home with me!"* To which I replied, *"Me TOO!"* We squealed like little school girls; Daniel smiled and shook his head. She then went through his grades and told us that it was "very clear" that *"Cole gets a lot of support and encouragement at home from the both of you, and he is doing very well as a result."* Awesomesauce.

Now my big boy. Jason. He is the reason for the season. Woo Hoo! Honestly, if the truth be told, I could have really screwed this child UP. Royally. I mean really. Three divorces? Several schools? Long commutes? Who would really blame that baby if he smoked cigarettes in his draws all day and played video games with children in Russia for a living?? Nope. Nope. Nope.

He graduated from high school with an Advanced Studies diploma, and all of his family came together: Me, Clarence, his wife, Daniel and all his grandparents, siblings and cousins. We had an amazing graduation lunch at a Washington Harbor hotel restaurant, overlooking the Potomac River. Clarence's wife and I worked together to make it special and Jason was beaming the entire day. This fall was his first semester of college at Virginia Commonwealth University.

And, by all accounts, he was successful! I have no grandchildren in training; no clinic visits; I didn't have to attend any support groups with him AND he didn't flunk a class. Hooray! Go Jason! Its' ya birthday! Hey Hey Hey! I knew he had crossed over into maturity land about a month into school. He told me that he knew he was starting to go to sleep too late, so he sets his alarm clock at 11:30pm...to go to bed! What? Is this MY child? God is so good!!

On the professional front, the skies are blue too. In January, Michael and I brought Ralph Samson into our firm. The fellas worked together for many years in construction management and property acquisition, with Michael spearheading the real estate component and Ralph handling the legal aspects. We knew that our firm could really get off the ground with us working together, and sure enough, it did. We ended the year with several large contracts. By partnering with amazing people of different backgrounds, I learn more and more everyday about synergy and the value of collaboration.

Separately, I have built up my brand as a small business advocate. In the last year, I have solidified my relationship with the Small Business Administration as both a mentor for SCORE and an instructor with its Emerging Leaders program—a six month course that facilitates existing business owners to develop their strategic growth plans. I'm also a contributing writer for *Black Enterprise* and *American Express OPEN Forum* — that was very exciting! And I finally fulfilled my high school and college dream of being in front of the news camera. I do monthly small business segments on *Fox 5 Morning News and NewsChannel 8,* and I love, love, love it! All small business. All different aspects. All phenomenal experiences.

Another part of that kick-ass year was becoming President of the DC Metro Chapter of the Twelve Days of Christmas. Remember earlier when I was so nervous about whether I was "enough" to be in the organization? Well, I encouraged myself to step up and serve in a leadership role for the first time ever.

This is a great story of love and spiritual growth for me. Why? I didn't realize it but, I was "afraid" of women, and I believed that the ladies wouldn't like me, so I stayed within my shell for many years. After working out all those insecurities, I challenged myself and accepted the nomination to become president. In 2015, our events have been the most highly attended and we received the most donations ever on record. But, on a personal level, the ladies in the organization have been so supportive and encouraging. They regularly said how they loved my "enthusiasm" and "excited leadership"! It was such a blessing. I was experiencing another kind of love here as well by just being myself and being open and taking a chance. It has been wonderful.

I think that a huge highlight of the year was that I was asked to speak at the *"World of a Woman Conference"* in Cairo, Egypt last November! It was an amazing opportunity to meet women from all around the world and talk about entrepreneurship and women's leadership. In my speech, I shared my journey. I told them about the young woman who came to DC to follow her passion, only to get kicked on her ass a few times while trying to make a life for herself. I told the story of how Soul opened and closed. I told the story of how I turned the page and began a new chapter as a small business advocate and empowerment coach.

When I finished, I got the most heartfelt hugs and handshakes. Many thanked me for my honesty and courage; some said they were going through it too! One woman thanked me for sharing about my divorce and child custody struggles because there in Cairo, she was experiencing the same thing. That exchange took my breath away. We are not as different as we think. And when we share our experiences instead of live in the shame of them, we heal.

That trip created the fuel I needed to complete this book. I had been trying to write and finish this book for many years. I started journaling soon after I closed Soul. But I wasn't ready. I still had some more living to do, you know? More healing. More growing. And I know God's hand was here all along, scripting it all.

. . .

And oh, just one more thing. Michael proposed to me recently. I wanted to share that with you too! He was supposed to go with me to Cairo (where he was going to propose), but had to cancel because of a business conflict. And one evening we were binge watching *How to Get Away with Murder* in my apartment. We dozed off and woke up at around 1am and watched the latest episode. And then, he turned off the TV and after sitting for a moment in the dimly lit room, he played Jeffery Osborne's "We're Going All The Way" on his iPhone and sat it down on the ottoman...He opened a beautifully wrapped, small golden box. In that box was the most beautiful ring I'd ever seen. He got down on one knee...and my eyes erupted like two mini sprinkler systems. I was crying so much that I couldn't hear what he said clearly, but Jeffery said it perfectly:

> *We're just beginning*
> *And I know we've each been down this road a time or two*
> *And never could make it through*
> *But I've got this feelin'*
> *That we've stumbled in to what we've both been waiting for*
> *And maybe even more*
> *It doesn't matter where we've been 'cause this time I know for sure*
>
> *. . .*
>
> *I know for certain*
> *That there's more than magic in these feelings that we found*
> *We're standin' on solid ground*
> *But now we're both ready*
> *Ready for the real thing 'cause our dues have all been paid*
> *We've finally got it made*
> *Believe me when I tell you there's no need to be afraid*

We're goin' all the way (All the way)
We're headed for forever and that's where we're gonna
stay...

I believe I have known that this type of love could exist since I was that 6 year old girl in kindergarten, opening her little heart to her classmate. But what I realized is that love exists everywhere only when you have the courage to learn how to love yourself first and completely. When I overcame my own insecurities and opened my heart, not in a needy, desperate way, but in a, as my "friend" the author Brené Brown says, wholehearted way, the results dramatically changed. I needed to make sure that my "cup" was full first — that I was healthy, and happy and...enough. Only I was responsible for that process.

In the past, I felt that relationships or accomplishments were the gateway to validation and happiness. That's where I went wrong. I learned that I was enough, simply because God made me. If He loved me without condition, it gave me the courage to do the same! Once I genuinely received that gift, then I started attracting such positive energy and love; not only from Michael, but from my sisters in my organization as well as women around the world. (Oh and on FB — social media love is cool too! Lol) By Loving God, Loving Myself and then Loving Others (in that order), I really created an entire new life for myself. I'm immensely grateful for my journey and am looking forward to the next chapter. Thanks for taking the time to read my story.

THE END...and THE BEGINNING!

Acknowledgements

I am sincerely grateful for every person who appeared on a page in my life, i.e. the book. Each person presented me with an opportunity to love, to live, and/or to hurt...but they all helped me to grow.

I want to again acknowledge Barbara and Andre Cober. The amount of unconditional love and support that my parents have given me through the peaks and valleys of my life fortified me with the strength to eventually *"love myself a little bit more"* and to give to others in an authentic way.

My children are simply brilliant, funny, and gracious young men. My most important role on Earth is to love, educate and raise these fellas to know their value and purpose. Boys: Your light gives me LIFE! I simply cannot wait to see how God's gifts will manifest through your lives.

I have had the breathtaking support of my many sister/brother friends who have had my back and heart throughout the writing of this book. Brandon C., Rachelle C., The LeBlanc Family, especially my beloved second mother, Maude (1934-2015), Fred C., Nari W., Karima M.A., Charlisa E., Lita A., Tenise J., Jeff W., John C., Kathey P., Dorothy M., Nicole C., Scott H., Kris P., Errika J., Nicole E., Robin F., Karen S., Kellye and Mike C., Karen T., Adriane K., Ricci and Karen J., LaShawn E, Stacy B., Kemit M., Chet J., Ila B., Pam M., Denise S., my church family at First Baptist Chesterbrook, Invictus 10, Teri H., my Delta Sigma Theta Sorority, Inc. sorors and my Twelve Days of Christmas, Inc. sisters.

To My Extended Team who were instrumental in creating the "CEO Of My SOUL" machine: Tamara Holmes, Lani Furbank, JR Arthur, the folks at Infusionsoft, Cameron Tyler, Cedric Terrell, Tiffany Lumpkin, LaShae Mclean and Aisha McCray.

Thanks to my family at NewsChannel 8, namely Courtney Gwynn, Glen Batte, and Kellye Lynn; Fox5 Morning News, namely Kenicia Cross and Micheline Bowman, Black Enterprise, the Greater Washington Urban League and American Express OPEN Forum, SCORE and my Emerging Leaders family for all the support you have given me. You have not only helped me be an advocate for the small business owner, you helped me use my experiences to turn the page and start an amazing new chapter in my life.

To my amazing law firm partners, Harold W. Johnson, II and Norman Romney. You are the best friends and partners this lady could have.

To all the small business owners. You are the heartbeat that wakes America up daily. You are rock stars.

To Oakland, for fortifying me with Town Strength — it's an armor that can never be broken.

To "My Koinonos"...thank you for existing, for supporting and for inspiring me. You are the daily manifestation God's love for me.

To My Heavenly Father. Thank you for your patience, love, friendship and for giving me a strong *soul.*

About The Author

Nic Cober, Esquire is the Principal Managing Partner of Cober Johnson & Romney, a law firm in Washington, DC. Her practice group focuses on small business advocacy and includes business and media consulting for the small business owner. She is also an instructor for the Emerging Leaders program and a mentor at SCORE, both affiliated with the Small Business Administration. Further, Ms. Cober is a regular contributor to Black Enterprise, American Express OPEN Forum, NewsChannel 8 and Fox 5 Morning News.

Ms. Cober is a graduate of University of California, Berkeley (Mass Communications and Sociology) and Howard University School of Law. She was also a law clerk for the DC Court of Appeals and a former associate of Dickstein Shapiro. She owned and operated Soul...Day Spa and Salon, a chain of small businesses for nearly a decade before opening her current law firm.

Ms. Cober is the mother of two sons and is recently engaged. She loves, yoga, brunches, wine festivals, cupcakes and music for the *soul*...

CPSIA information can be obtained
at www.ICGtesting.com
Printed in the USA
FFOW04n0542180117
31454FF